This book is about meaningful culture change, individual and organizational learning, leadership humanity and resilience, and organizational excellence. It documents a long, challenging, but totally inspirational account of multiple plants' transformations, but also provides a unique window into a boss-subordinate relationship that is textured, real, and uplifting. Women in leadership (way beyond manufacturing) will be interested in this account of gifted, yet humble leadership. I am challenged to convey how much I loved the content and style of this book.

– Jane Dutton, Professor of Psychology and Business Administration Emerita, University of Michigan

Kathy and Shannon are systems-based thinkers which makes their Lean Enterprise implementation successful and sustainable. Understanding their journey and challenges makes this book a must read for both new lean thinkers and seasoned lean professionals.

– Rick Harris, President of Harris Lean Systems, Inc.

Kathy and Shannon offer a glimpse of the struggles and barriers they have faced on their road to a successful Lean transformation. It would behoove all leaders to truly understand these obstacles and perspectives through their eyes so that the unique traits of both genders meld into synergistic, winning organizations. This breakthrough publication is required reading if one is serious about building a diverse, world-class organization.

– Mark DeLuzio, President & CEO Lean Horizons Consulting, Shingo Prize Academy Inductee

Kathy and Shannon's management principles go beyond the manufacturing sector. This book is more than techniques and tools, it is about people. It is about how you connect, engage and build trust. It speaks to the heart of business leaders.

– Maureen Donker, Mayor, City of Midland, Michigan; Executive Director, Reece Endeavor of Midland

Not only a technically sound lean transformation, but a story of leadership, friendship, and camaraderie. These ladies demonstrate strength through vulnerability, perseverance through compassion, and remind us all of what true leadership looks like.

– Diane M. Larkin: Executive Vice President Global Operations, Valmont Industries

This is an inspiring and important story – one that is deeply relevant today, with timeless principles for both women and men, seasoned professionals, and those just starting their careers. It is a story of courageous women, working side by side with the masters of lean manufacturing to transform a business. It is the story of how they built an inclusive culture where teams felt connected, engaged, and trusted. Through their rigorous and fulfilling work, they delivered for their employees, employer, and stakeholders alike.

– Roger Lehman, Managing Partner, Oliver Wyman

Don't be fooled by the shoes. With an unapologetically female voice, Kathy and Shannon take you down to the plant floor and show you what it really takes to execute a lean transformation.

– Angie Tuglus, Executive Advisor

This is a fascinating autobiographical account of two women manufacturing leaders spearheading a successful lean transformation. Authors Kathy and Shannon share their stories of shaping team culture on the shop floor, battling workplace microaggressions and outright sexism, and balancing family life with courage, determination, and poise. Their friendship offers a refreshing take on women supporting each other's success in the workplace. This book is an honest and easy read. Highly recommended for women aspiring to succeed in male-dominated professions.

– Meg Warren, Associate Professor of Management, Western Washington University

Steel Toes and Stilettos

Steel Toes and Stilettos

A True Story of Women Manufacturing Leaders and Lean Transformation Success

Shannon Karels and Kathy Miller

CRC Press
Taylor & Francis Group
Boca Raton London New York

CRC Press is an imprint of the
Taylor & Francis Group, an **informa** business
A PRODUCTIVITY PRESS BOOK

Illustrations and cover design by Seana Ozinga.

First published 2022
by Routledge
605 Third Avenue, New York, NY 10158

and by Routledge
2 Park Square, Milton Park, Abingdon, Oxon, OX14 4RN
Routledge is an imprint of the Taylor & Francis Group, an informa business

Library of Congress Cataloging-in-Publication Data

A catalog record for this title has been requested

ISBN: 9781032053110 (hbk)
ISBN: 9781032053103 (pbk)
ISBN: 9781003196976 (ebk)

DOI: 10.4324/9781003196976

Typeset in Garamond
by Deanta Global Publishing Services, Chennai, India

To
Scott Karels
and
Jeff Miller

Our husbands
Best friends
Greatest champions

Contents

Foreword

Kathy and Shannon's freshman debut is a must-read for any leader (not just female leaders!) looking to improve business performance, team dynamics, and interpersonal leadership skills.

As leaders and mentors, we all look for that colleague that we can vent to, share stories with, and learn from, and the authors have beautifully created that colleague for the reader in this book. Not like your typical "how-to" management book that reads more like a college textbook, *Steel Toes and Stilettos* is an extremely enjoyable read with a wonderful balance of endearing stories, expert advice, real grounding examples, and tangible tips that any leader can use with their teams. This leadership guide reads more like a summer novel with the humorous, relatable, and real approach the authors have taken with the narrative. I found myself going back to sections, because I wanted to hear the experience again. I wanted to reconnect to the story the writers were telling and find my bond to the event. So many times, as a leader, you hold yourself more accountable than anyone else can and you struggle with your failures. This book helped me appreciate the trials and tribulations of my career and made me think of them as lessons along my journey to being a better leader. You will pick up a few tips and tricks throughout the book, but most importantly I think you will find the story of a genuine partnership to be inspiring. This special bond and trust is what we should all strive for in our professional relationships and, as you will see in the book, is the magic recipe for the OPSisters' success. You can have the best processes in the world, but if you don't have the hearts and minds of your people, that success cannot be sustained. So sit back, kick off your shoes, and get ready to devour one of the most enjoyable leadership stories you have ever read!

Darcy Robison, *Senior Director Social Responsibility*

Preface

As we started writing this book, we realized that it could be many things for many people. Ultimately it is a story – a story of two women in the workplace who have succeeded in a male-dominated industry, who refused to be anything other than ourselves as women, professionals, and leaders. It is a true story of how we led a manufacturing business through a successful lean transformation.

We also reflected on who would read this book and why they would read it. We initially wrote it for that young female in or around manufacturing. We wanted to inspire her through our story. We want to be successful role models that may look or act or think like her. We acknowledged that this type of positive female influence was missing for us when we started our careers. We also wanted to share some "how-to" tips to give her a leg up on the competition. (Nothing wrong with that!)

We also hope it will be a case study for all of those who champion inclusivity in the workplace. We had so many men who were mentors, coaches, and allies for us along the way. We hope it will provide inspiration to those who serve in that capacity for others and for those who aspire to create a future for businesses that value diversity of thought.

It is a story about a female executive (Kathy) responsible for a business's profitability and all the lives that the company supports, both within its walls and among their family members. It is a story about a high-potential female employee (Shannon) who worked her way up to become a leadership team member because of her accomplishments and potential to significantly contribute to the success of the business. It is a story of how we met, developed a high-performing team, and transformed multiple plants into a lean enterprises, with all the accompanying business performance improvements. It is a story of our friendship – how it grew from mere business acquaintances to sisterhood.

It is also a leadership book – leadership that is authentic and nontraditional. It is about how we created a positive environment where every employee could bring their very best to the work world every day.

Finally, this book could also be read as a "how-to" book for that traditional lean transformation so many businesses attempt to implement. Our story demonstrates how making this transformation not only improves key performance metrics but also enables a culture that is safe, is inclusive, and drives value for the customer. We will share the steps and what we learned along the way, including some of those hard lessons and some of the great things we stumbled upon that helped accelerate the journey.

There are many books out there on how to "do lean" with various tools and principles. While we will describe some of the tools that we implemented in both the manufacturing plants and the office, our journey was more than the techniques and tools. It was about the people. It was about how we connected with them, how we engaged them, and how we built trust in the challenging world in which we operated. It is difficult but truly critical if you aspire to create a place where people flourish, and business results are exceptional.

We have written this book together but also include our personal perspectives of the journey. We have different roles, personalities, and perspectives that add to the authenticity of the struggles and the triumphs we experienced. We also share a glimpse of what was going on in our lives outside of work to reinforce that life is full of many experiences that shape us, not just our careers. We believe that our support in each other both professionally and personally throughout this journey contributed to the excellent results and, more importantly, our enduring friendship. We hope that our story will inspire other "OPSisters."

Acknowledgments

The idea for this book was developed in a most untraditional way – on a family weekend together, in a hot tub, with a bottle of champagne. We believe many of the world's problems (or maybe just ours) can be solved in this fashion. When some great business deals are done on golf courses, beer in hand, why couldn't they be generated in a hot tub with a different sort of beverage?!

As we sipped and savored some cherished memories of transforming multiple plants into lean enterprises, we had an epiphany – what happened along that journey was actually quite remarkable. That realization was followed by, "We should really tell people about this." And, "Maybe someone could learn something from our unconventional approach!" The next day we had a title for our story, and within one year, we had written a manuscript. The process of writing this book generated yet another set of memories we will fondly cherish for years to come. It also provided insight into how our different personalities and strengths complemented one another. And, when we didn't even think it was possible, it further solidified our sister-like friendship.

As we have learned throughout our careers, nothing is accomplished alone, and we have had the most amazing group of people who have helped us bring our story to life. Our relationships run wide and deep, and our hearts are filled with enormous gratitude. A big thank you to all our friends and family, both inside and outside of work (we tend to blend the two) that have supported us through this project and our careers. You know who you are, and we are so blessed to have you in our lives.

We are especially grateful to our parents, Greg and Diane Fishel (Kathy's) and Michael and Marie McCall and Joanne and John Onderko (Shannon's), for raising us with so much love and instilling in us courage, confidence, and the value of hard work. We are also appreciative to those who call us "Mom": Emily Haza and Claire McCombs (Kathy's daughters), and Beckett Karels (Shannon's son). Your unconditional love for and patience with us (especially during extended time in front of a computer screen) mean the world to us.

We would also like to offer thanks to those who offered specific support and encouragement for this project. Each one of you wore a different type of shoe that supported our journey! So, thank you, Taylor Allen, Tracy Albrecht, Leona Brandwene, Heidi Brown, Tom Carbon, Mark DeLuzio, Nathan Haza, Rebecca Fleetwood Hession, Tom Karels, Devin Longo, Alyssa Miller, Jennifer Miller, Michelle Miller, Seana Ozinga, Alex Perry, and Angie Tuglus.

We are appreciative to Michael Sinocchi and Productivity Press with Routledge Taylor & Francis Group for taking a chance on this project with first-time authors and helping us tell this type of story in a nontraditional way.

To our content editor, Karli Jackson, we thank you for powering through our first draft and providing incredibly insightful feedback.

Lastly, thank you to Rick Harris, our teacher, coach, "tough-love" provider, and mentor. You were by our side every step of the way through this story we share.

Authors

Shannon Karels is a Senior Operations Manager, who has led multiple lean transformations and run operations for two large publicly traded corporations across multiple industries and business models. She started her career in supply chain management and progressed through lean and operations leadership roles. Through this journey, Shannon has improved cultures in numerous manufacturing facilities by leading employee empowerment and engagement and building highly successful teams, with a focus on business results. Shannon is known for leading accountable organizations built on trusting relationships that improve the companies' profitability and customer experience. Shannon holds a Bachelor's Degree in Supply Chain Management from Western Michigan University.

Kathy Miller is a Senior Operations Executive, who has held numerous Global Vice President and Director roles both in manufacturing and lean enterprise leadership. Kathy is a Shingo Prize Recipient for Large Businesses as a Plant Manager. She started her career in operations as a 17-year-old co-op student at a vehicle assembly plant and progressed through engineering, marketing, lean manufacturing, and operations leadership roles, working for four large publicly traded corporations in executive roles. Kathy is a transformational leader who consistently delivers impressive business results through team development, process discipline, and continuous improvement. Kathy is known for the creation of inclusive cultures based on trust, respect, and accountability. Kathy holds a Bachelor of Science Degree in Industrial and Systems Engineering from Kettering University (formerly GMI Engineering and Management Institute), a Master's Degree in Business Administration from Ball State University, and a Master's Degree in Applied Positive Psychology from the University of Pennsylvania.

Introduction

The authors professionally joined forces when Kathy hired Shannon to be a part of her divisional leadership team – responsible for a $75 m operation with hundreds of team members at four locations in two countries. This book is about the journey they went on to transform a traditionally run batch operation to a Lean enterprise – characterized by authentic leadership, an inclusive culture, and excellent business results.

The book not only outlines the steps of the transformational journey but emphasizes the softer sides of the implementation process. It will highlight some of the challenges and triumphs along the way and how they overcame them. Kathy and Shannon share the fun and emotion of the three years and the endearing friendship that was formed along the way from each of their perspectives. Kathy's perspective is from an executive position with profit and loss responsibility, while Shannon's is from the Lean leader responsible for the transformation.

Kathy and Shannon share anecdotes from their personal lives during the transformation to show relatability with how real life still happens and requires attention while working hard to get effective business results. In addition, they detail experiences of being women working in a male-dominated industry, what that meant to them, and how they handled this environment.

This story will inspire women who are on that journey – it provides an example of how high-performing women can thrive in an intense and fast-paced world where you are judged to be as good as the performance of your organization 30 days at a time. Kathy and Shannon strive to be role models for those who are juggling dual-career marriages, raising families, and intense and fulfilling careers. All readers benefit from the adoption of the strategies and tools they used to facilitate this business transformation.

Essentially, this book can be read as a narrative account or used as an implementation guide for a Lean transformation. It shares some of the organizational and cultural roadblocks that arise during the implementation and how the authors overcame them. It focuses on their journeys both professionally and personally and shows the reader how women can work together to drive positive culture and business change in an organization.

1

Baby Shoes – *How It All Started*

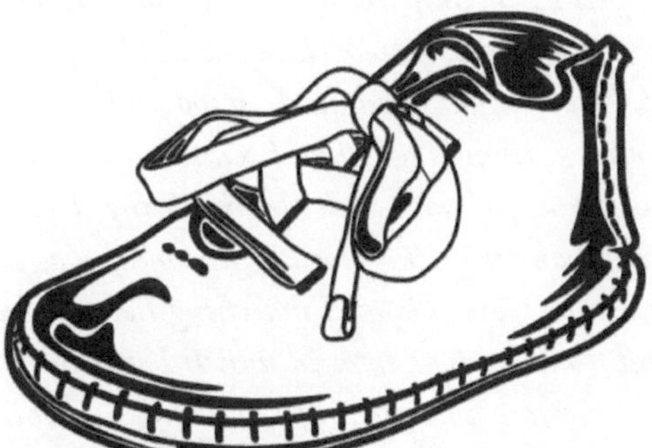

We all know that babies crawl before they walk and then walk before they run, so we begin our story with the image of baby shoes, as the lean journey we will lead you through was truly in its infancy. We will draw upon shoes to capture the stages of this business transformation, not only because they make for a great analogy but also because we love shoes. We adore not only the fabulous high-heeled ones that make a statement when you enter the room but also the gritty, grimy industrial safety shoes designed to protect you from all kinds of danger lurking inside factory walls. These safety shoes exclaim, "I am here, factory friends, and I belong here!"

Lean manufacturing has been around for decades and started in the automotive industry. It is a methodology for creating value for the customer, providing what they want when they want it. Lean methods focus on eliminating waste and creating an inclusive environment where all employees contribute to solving problems. It is process-oriented and aimed at creating the flow of information, people, and material. The concepts are used in all types of businesses, although the tools were developed for manufacturing first and then adapted.

Our story takes place primarily in manufacturing plants and the surrounding functions: finance, marketing, human resources, and so on. The business we were responsible for consisted of four plants in two different countries. This story describes our two U.S. plants' transformations with a brief view of our Mexico plant's efforts. We eventually transformed the fourth plant as well, but we will save that story for the sequel. So, strap on your boots, or cuddle up in some comfy slippers, and come along with us.

DOI: 10.4324/9781003196976-1

Kathy

My love affair with car plants started when I was a ripe age of 17 years old. It was not love at first sight. I had been accepted at a small private engineering college, one that required half of my college years working in a company gaining real-life experience and half of the time in traditional classroom education. The company that sponsored most of the students at this institution of higher learning had a vehicle assembly plant 15 miles from where I lived. Since I had barely obtained my driver's license when I was called to interview for one of the few coveted co-op positions, my dad drove me to the plant. After my four hours of interviews, which took place in the front offices, I was asked if I would like to take a tour of the plant and if the man in the lobby who had been waiting all day would like to join us. I politely accepted for myself and invited my dad.

As we stepped through a sizeable beige door, a "people door," a term I learned later, we entered a whole new world – the world of the vehicle assembly line. It was loud. The floors were black and made of woodblocks. People worked in pits in some areas, appearing as though they had been truncated at the waist. Train tracks were running through, as in, not beside, the building. I had never seen anything like it. I saw very few women in the plant. I assume I was somewhat of a novel sight in my navy blue interview suit and matching heels. I was accompanied by Human Resources and a man whose arm in which I was overtly intertwined. This evoked all sorts of commotion, consisting of whistling, whooping, and hollering. As I came to understand later, this was a tour for beginners. My father and I were guided through main aisles, away from the inner sanctum of the areas where the calendars of naked women and unsavory graffiti decorated toolboxes, columns, and walls.

As my dad was the most protective of fathers when it came to his daughter, I concluded the tour confident that he would not ever want me to go back there. We didn't chat very much on the way home; we just shared some peanut M&M's he kept in his glove box for good measure. The next day, Human Resources called and offered me a job at the plant in Industrial Engineering. I asked them to please hold the phone while I consulted with my dad, who did not even hesitate for one second before answering, "just accept it." "What about how rough the place was, Daddy, with the catcalls and whistling … and that was when ***you*** *were by my side???" "Oh," he said, brushing off the concern, "that was harmless; you'll be fine." And so, it began.*

After five years of alternating between school and work, a rigorous engineering curriculum, and stints in nearly every plant department, I grew up quickly. I learned about Thermodynamics and Operations Research and how ***not*** *to wear my heart on my shirtsleeve and do time studies without carrying a stopwatch. The year I graduated, the plant closed after 50 years in operation, and I, along with the rest of the plant personnel, followed the last car down the line. It was an extremely sad experience that taught me that nothing in business is a sure thing. I would need to continue to develop my skills and knowledge so I would have options in the future.*

I transferred to another location within the same company, two states away, went back into Engineering, and started my MBA classes at night. In those Engineering and Marketing years, I did not have to pack both office and plant shoes, as my duties confined me to the world of cubicles. I did, however, still have a big decision to make regarding my footwear. It is a decision that every female professional faces eventually. It is a significant choice, one that will contribute to your personal brand – one that you will be judged by, either consciously or subconsciously. And so, this is how I made mine.

I stood in my closet, which was in a state of transition from stirrup pants and shoulder-padded, knee-length sweaters to the world of a professional wardrobe which called for structured trousers, matching blazers, and blouses that required ironing. I took it all in. There were fat pants, skinny pants, pants hemmed appropriately for high heels, and another set, same category, same colors, just hemmed to a different length for flat shoes. There were just too many combinations. Simplifying was not an option; it was a necessity. As a serial crash dieter, I knew the charts all too well, how tall I should be for my given weight. And, so, I took a deep breath and made the decision. I would no longer alternate between flats and heels. I was going to be a high-heel girl. I would eventually weed out pants hemmed for short heels. I needed the height. I would be that professional who carried herself with three extra inches, in pants or skirts, no matter where my job would take me.

My early professional career alternated between Engineering and Marketing for different automotive electronic product lines. In those years, I continued to progress upward through the organization, acquiring more responsibility. I got married and gave birth to two baby girls, 4.5 years apart. After my second daughter was born, I found that I missed plant life and returned to manufacturing, progressing through a Superintendent position and into a Plant Operations Manager position, which had long been my ambition. During a stint between those two positions, I joined a team to deploy lean manufacturing throughout our company's operations. I learned about this manufacturing system from many of the people who wrote the early lean operations books.

Shortly after my automotive electronics plant won the Shingo Prize for its lean transformation and business results, I left automotive. I joined a diversified industrial company as the Lean Manager, of an organization about $2B in size. Having done lean while running thousands of car parts a day gave me instant credibility with my peers, leaders responsible for the various divisions' profitability. I traveled around to each location, getting to know their teams and their business challenges. I set up workshops, facilitated improvement sessions, and coached their internal lean and manufacturing people. I understood that not all the challenges could be answered directly by what the books defined. Thinking was indeed required, and unfortunately, the pressures of day-to-day delivery would ALWAYS take precedence over whatever improvement event had been scheduled. I could work with that. I loved being a business partner with those General Managers. We developed great relationships – some more challenging than others, but if they shot straight with me, we were okay. We worked **on** the business together, enabling them to work **in** the business with better results.

This early success led to me being promoted to the Vice President (VP) of Lean Enterprise and Quality for the entire corporation within six months of *joining the company. It would have happened a month or two sooner, but they wanted me to move to the Corporate Headquarters, 315 miles away. That wasn't possible. The other pair of shoes that I wore in those days were those of a divorced mom with joint custody of my two daughters. I had promised my girls that I would always have a home within 10 miles of where their dad lived so we could raise them together, even though we lived in separate houses. I would not go back on my promise to those little girls for any promotion. So, after the third ask for me to relocate, and my third time turning down the position, it was decided I could stay where I was and do the job if I were willing to travel. My ex-husband and I worked very well together to make sure we both had our quality time with the girls. With the flexibility that afforded me, I was able to accept the promotion.*

My responsibilities increased from $2 billion in revenue to $12 billion. I inherited a lean system with well-defined visual management tools and a team of lean professionals that worked by my side, creating the balance of the operating system. We taught it throughout the company worldwide, from the CEO through the shop floor team members. It was rigorous and fulfilling work.

I worked in that role for five years, personally visiting over 200 plants in more than 20 countries. I was very proud of the work accomplished in this role. We had developed the operating system for both manufacturing and non-manufacturing processes, taught it worldwide, and helped implement it in over 120 divisions and more than 300 plants around the globe. We created and launched a quality strategy, eliminated fork trucks everywhere except in the warehouses, improved company productivity by 30%, and reduced inventory by 15%, among other achievements.

These industrial plants were a bit more rigorous than the automotive electronics plants, so I finally had to adopt safety shoes as a main staple in my wardrobe. I added them to my packing checklist and made room for them in my suitcases. Except, sometimes, I forgot, or there really wasn't enough space in my bag, and so it was, this is how I first met Shannon.

I was doing an audit at a plant in Illinois, and I showed up without my safety shoes. As I came to appreciate my role in setting the example for safety, I never tried to get into the plants without them anymore. This predicament became my first encounter with her. After the introductory presentation had concluded, I let the Plant Manager know that I needed to borrow a pair. After examining the assortment of men's shoes kept for visitors, Shannon came forward and offered me hers. How fortunate (or maybe even fortuitous) that we wear the same size! So, I donned her shoes, which resembled brown laced-up hiking boots, and went on the tour. Who'd have known that first meeting would mark the beginning of a journey, a journey of professional accomplishments, a journey of sisterhood, just without the shared DNA.

A couple of years after I visited that plant in Illinois, it was time for me to get off the road, so I took a job as the General Manager of one of the company's divisions. I had been to this division a few times in my previous role, so I knew a bit of what to expect. My first day there was planned by my boss, a day of team presentations and a plant tour. I remember it well – most of it spent in a conference room, the walls sporting c. 1970s' wood paneling. This paneling was not the solid, stately boardroom kind that encompasses you with a feeling that you are in the presence of greatness. It was the flat simulated wood type that is hung in sheets, making it a widely available material to even the most novice of hammer-wielding carpenters, mostly called "Dad."

The plant tour of this first day felt a little different from my new vantage point as the new leader. Maybe it was because I was more observant about every single thing my path crossed, not just the level of lean maturity I had previously evaluated. The vintage equipment was large and industrial, and it was much darker and dirtier than I had recalled. Stalactites of soot hung from the ceiling. I remembered the jokes about the casket gaskets produced there (never got any customer complaints) and the chicken plucker fingers that helped remove feathers from varieties of poultry being prepared for human consumption. The plant looked a lot different, and the jokes were not so funny now that it was my responsibility.

The corner office, which I had worked so hard to finally occupy, was outfitted with a desk that people were afraid to put their legs under for fear of it collapsing and causing a recordable injury. This desk and the carpeting on which it rested predated the sheet-paneled conference room upgrades by about a decade.

I was ready to be in an operational role again, but I felt a LOT of pressure – pressure to succeed as a General Manager to prove that I could successfully run a business' profit and loss in a male-dominated world. There were 3 other women running divisions out of approximately 120 at the time. I was also juggling many time-consuming items on the home front. My new husband (of three years) and I decided to buy a home near my new workplace as I couldn't make the 2.5-hour commute daily. The real estate market in the area was unpredictably complicated and frustrating. I was also negotiating a buyback with a car dealer on a new vehicle that was unfortunately a lemon.

My oldest daughter was in her senior year of high school, and I had long been traumatized about her growing up and leaving me. I was driving back and forth very frequently on weekdays to partake in all of the Senior activities, acutely aware that this was the last Honor Roll Recognition Program, the last Show Choir Concert, the final Orchestra Concert. It was that period of life I had dreaded since she was nine years old, playing on the swing set. I remember looking over at her from the swing I was on as she was about to go down the slide, thinking, "I can't believe this is halfway over."

During these early transition days, I needed to get my new leadership team together. I learned that the Divisional Controller and Engineering Director had chosen to transfer to another location with my predecessor. This detail had been conveniently not mentioned when I accepted the position. So, I had to get financial and engineering leadership for the team quickly. The 30-day cycles of production and financial accounting are unrelenting, and none of the requirements of running an operation were paused for the organizational challenges needing resolution. I juggled all of it – outwardly courageous and self-assured, inwardly spinning, all the while my new team members assessing their new leader.

I also needed to turn my attention to hiring a Lean Manager. My instincts told me I had about 18 months before the Senior Operations Executive would show up to see if I could really do a lean transformation versus just teaching others how to do it. Time was of the essence.

I had arrived at my new division in March. In May, I got a call from shoe-loaning Shannon. She was looking for her next career opportunity. She wanted to stay in Chicago, had heard that I was looking for a Lean Manager, and she was interested in applying for the position. My largest and most profitable plant was in Chicago, so I was open to her living in a different location. After all, one of my other staff members was there, so it wasn't like my whole team of direct reports would be sitting with me around a conference room table every week. As we've already discussed, none of the conference rooms had awe-inspiring library paneling anyway. I remember thinking that anyone who was brave enough to come work for the ex-VP of Lean to implement lean deserved a shot. And, she had loaned me her steel toes that time.

I asked her to send me her resume. It was great. She was a proper Supply Chain professional. Since material flow, which is driven by information flow, should be coming from the Supply Chain team or the "brains of the operation," as we liked to call them, I was sure she would do well. She had been one of the first Supply Chain Trainees hired by the corporation. She had completed several rotational assignments before landing her full-time opportunity and was doing quite well. She was the personification of what intern development programs are all about.

While there is no documented hiring process for divisional staff positions that I could identify, it was broadly understood that your candidate choice must be approved one layer above you and by the functional owner (one's dotted line boss – #matrixlife). So, Shannon went through the interview process with me and various members of my leadership team. She then was vetted by my boss and her corresponding functional boss. My Human Resources Manager was about to make the offer when I was informed that Shannon must go through an additional battery of interviewers never required for any other comparable position before or since this one was filled, to my knowledge. I am a process person. If I weren't before college, I certainly became one as part of my Industrial Engineering education. Since this didn't seem to be following any "standard" protocol, I was a bit frustrated.

The additional interviewer from the Corporate Human Resources team expressed concern that Shannon did not have a lean background nor had she indicated on her "Career Interest Form" that she desired to be in this Lean Manager role. Clearly, the "Career Interest Form" had somewhere along the way become a sacred document, and all moves in this global corporation were to be facilitated by strict adherence to the employee's wishes documented therein. After some deep breathing, corporate wrangling, and a mini-meltdown about choosing my own team, particularly in the function where I was considered the "corporate expert," Shannon and I were awarded an all-expense-paid trip to Corporate Headquarters, where

I attended an interview with Shannon, my boss, and the concerned Corporate Human Resources Manager. Shannon will relay her fond memories of this meeting with you shortly. My recollection of this three-hour interview was that it was conducted in a small office that was as hot as the blazes of Hell, and Shannon, in her business suit complimented by a pair of smart black pumps, hung in there like a champ. She displayed great staying power and grit. She was most definitely my girl for the job.

Shannon

My leadership story starts very early on when I found myself committed to the sport of gymnastics. In this challenging sport, which is physically and mentally gruelling, I learned so many of the fundamental values that would carry me through life. By practicing and coaching six hours a day after eight hours of school, I learned a lot about time management. I successfully figured out how to get my homework done and graduated from high school with honors. Even though gymnastics is mostly an individual sport, I found that I wanted to lead the team. I wanted to be a role model for my teammates, be an example of hard work and dedication. I was voted captain of the team, and so, my leadership journey began. I developed leadership skills, albeit rough skills. You have to start somewhere. I learned about risk-taking and what it was like to fail. And to lose. I knew I preferred to win so much more and worked very hard to do so. I had a gymnastics life and a school life. I found myself in the part of life where I had to make choices about college. I had to figure out what my future would entail. I knew I loved the sport and wanted to continue it. I also knew gymnastics would not be my professional career, and I had to choose an additional path.

I knew deep down that some aspect of business was my calling. I had created a business model for the school store in high school. I loved working with a team to create something that would attract people, make it easier to sell products, and increase revenue. I just thought it was fun. Who would have known that it would mean so much more? I decided to start a business degree at Western Michigan University and joined the gymnastics team. As I made my way through the general education track at Western, I stumbled into the Supply Chain profession by eliminating all the other business degree concentrations. My college advisor told me that there was a 98% job placement for women in Supply Chain. That sounded good to me, so I said, "Let's go for it!" It sounds all very spontaneous, but these were the days of the aftermath of 9/11. The world was never to be the same, the landscape of all of our futures uncertain. I, like much of the country, craved certainty and direction. I wanted to leave college with the best chance of secure employment. Supply Chain sounded like a great path.

Having decided on my major, I accepted a summer internship with a major automotive company, working in Purchasing and Packaging. This was my first experience of being away from home, separated from my family by multiple states, and truly learning how to be on my own. It was a struggle, but it was a great first look at corporate life and started to pave the way for what I would choose (or avoid) in my professional career. During this time, I also had to make a very tough decision regarding my gymnastics career. I had broken my foot and was experiencing a tremendous amount of back pain. I decided to end my involvement in the sport. It was one of the most difficult decisions I have ever made, as I am not a quitter; however, upon much soul-searching, it was the right one for my body and my mental health.

After leaving the world of gymnastics, I quickly learned why everyone thought college was so much fun! I started to partake in all sorts of activities that gymnastics had not allowed. I successfully finished those fourish years of study, with many tears, laughs, and great memories to take with me. That hard work and dedication served me well. I graduated with honors and was recruited by a Fortune 500 company.

The company was a diversified industrial manufacturing company, with approximately $12B in revenue. I was to be one of their first Supply Chain Trainees. The program consisted of a two-year training rotation for different assignments in various parts of the company. I got hands-on experience in real jobs in the Supply Chain functions, including logistics, purchasing, planning, and inventory management. It was a season of mixed emotions for me. I was so excited to receive the offer to join this select group of new college graduates. I was also sad about it taking me away from my family. Among my closest group of friends, I was one of the first to leave home. I would be assigned to different locations in different parts of the country every six months and didn't know upfront where those places were. I moved four times in those two years. With each move, I found myself alone. I had no family, no friends. It was also the first time I'd lived on my own for such a lengthy period, so there were a whole lot of sleepless nights.

I had to leave my comfort zone and force myself to meet new people. I am an introvert. I know it in my heart, and many a corporate assessment has confirmed it. I am very skilled at disguising my introversion in a familiar tight-knit inner circle. That is where I am an open book and a fiercely loyal friend. I am also a very comfortable public speaker, so people often don't realize how much energy it takes for me to be in large social groups. As a matter of survival, I needed to make friends in these new places. I so deeply wanted to be successful at this company, and navigating these new roles with the ever-changing cast of characters was key. I came to quickly realize that I could push myself through challenging situations, even working in that considerable distance from my comfort zone.

I started this new adventure in office roles where I upgraded my wardrobe to "business casual" and bought a few pairs of work-appropriate heels. (I had to interpret this term, as there were no guidelines for women as to what this term meant.) I, too, was height-challenged, and being in heels made me feel more confident, not to mention that I have enormous affection for stylish shoes! Part of the intern process is to discern what part of the vast Supply Chain array of roles was the most appealing. I quickly learned that I enjoyed being on the Operations side of the Supply Chain world. This led to the acquisition of multiple pairs of steel toe shoes and mornings of figuring out how to roll up and secure the hems of my dress pants to accommodate the lower heels of my safety shoes.

I was frequently asked by friends what was attractive about working in factories. I clearly had an affinity for high heels and nice clothing. I should be a fashion buyer or work in a marketing office. This career choice involved a more practical selection of footwear, as well as other personal protective equipment. I never did have a good answer. I just really enjoyed the challenge. I liked working on process improvements in the plants that made people's jobs easier. I loved collaborating with others and found satisfaction in solving parts of what seemed like a giant puzzle. I had never really known what I wanted to do with my career. I always felt a lot of pressure to articulate it and felt uncomfortable when those conversations arose. So, as I realized that I was pretty good at this, I started to gain confidence. As opportunities began opening up, it began to reinforce that I may have found my path.

Once I finished the two-year trainee program, I arrived at a significant decision point. What should I choose for my first full-time job? Where should I live? What type of business should I join that would be best for my career? How would my decision impact my family? Sometimes, having a lot of choices is more difficult than having none at all. Ultimately, I took a considerable risk and went to a division that was struggling. It had financial woes and problems with customer satisfaction. Their plan to fix the business was to embark on a lean journey. I thought this was an exciting endeavor and I could help drive the transformation. The division was located such that a visit to home was a drive, not a plane flight. As this opportunity was the perfect blend to meet all of my decision criteria, I chose this role. And, as a bonus, it should be noted that it involved both heels and steel toes!

I spent the next six years working in various Supply Chain roles, taking on more responsibility with each move. I was learning to be a leader and how to be much more patient with people. This was a critical time for my development. I'm grateful for those who tolerated my "enthusiasm" and put up with my aggressive pace. It was a time of significant growth, and I was fortunate to have a mentor who believed in me. He told me not to worry so much about the particular role I was in, that I was a leader. As long as I was leading people, I would be successful. I had never thought of my career that way, and with this endorsement and encouragement, I was able to relax and let hard work and my gut instincts be my guide.

There was a lot going on there – leadership changes and a lean transformation, both aimed to remedy monthly financial losses and low customer service levels. Through implementing the lean basics such as standard work, cell layout improvements, Plan-For-Every-Part (PFEP), part supermarkets, supplier pull systems, and material flow, we were able to improve customer delivery by 60% and profitability from the red to the black by over 20%, among so many other improvements. I bought into the concept of lean manufacturing and took it to heart as being the way to run a successful business.

During this time, I learned the power and importance of developing relationships and trust at all organizational levels. I knew I couldn't do everything alone and would only be as successful as the teams around me. I figured the best way to do that was to be honest, lead by example, and work hard, as I had in the past.

Being so young in my career, I learned how to navigate the business world, learning all of these new tools, concepts, and processes and realizing that being a young woman in manufacturing was far different from what I could have ever imagined. I didn't give up dressing nicely or wearing cute shoes in the office, and I didn't realize that being female in that environment meant something different than just being a person doing the best job to the best of their abilities. (In college, my perception was that the genders were created equally, and even in team environments, we played to each our strengths. I assumed this would remain the case in the business world.) I was told once, by my boss at that time, that I received accolades because the General Manager had a soft spot for girls. This was shocking to me since I figured it was just because I had done an excellent job. My view of this world started to change, and it took me time to figure out what that meant to me if anything.

In enters Kathy. The VP of Lean Enterprise and Quality, a female senior executive was coming to my plant. I was going to impress her and the rest of the team with the great things we had accomplished. After introductions, we had planned a plant tour. When I learned that she did not have steel toes with her, I immediately offered her mine, discovering that we have the same shoe size. From there, the tour was a bit of a blur. I remember Kathy spending a lot of time "explaining" that inventory triangles should never be on a future state value stream map (a lesson I have not since forgotten and used during my own subsequent "explaining" throughout value stream reviews). I remember being very impressed by her confidence and knowledge. I also discovered that I had a lot to learn.

A couple of years later, Kathy decided to move back into Operations to run a division, and I reached out to inquire about open opportunities. I was ready for my next role and had learned that she had a plant based in Chicago with a Lean Manager position open. I quickly applied. Coming from a Supply Chain degree and work experience, I felt it was a long shot, but going through that initial lean transformation was exciting. Who wouldn't want to jump into a lean role having never done it working for the previous VP of Lean (or the "Lean Queen" as I had heard her referred to by many)?

As Kathy mentioned, the interview process was lengthy, and I got to do a "bonus" interview to solidify the promotion. So, there we were being sweated out (literally) in a corporate office for hours while I tried my best to prove I could do this job. I was determined not to take that suit coat off, no matter how damn hot it was in there. I also had to take a personality assessment, which included many intrusive questions, and complete a personal interview by the outside company administering the assessment. The feedback I received was that I am very analytical and almost too logical (is that a thing?!?). I am a change agent and a task completer. This explained why and how I could enjoy solving these puzzles in fixing processes and getting things done. It was good timing and my skills complimented those required for this role.

While jumping through all these hoops and working my current job, I was also planning my wedding to my now-husband, Scott. That alone was a full-time job that consisted of yet another shoe dilemma, what type of footwear I should wear for the big day. A mutual friend of ours solved that dilemma by buying me a very expensive and beautiful pair of shoes that Kathy coveted and convinced me to keep. Who knew in these early days that yet more shoes would solidify our bond? Eventually, I made it through the gauntlet of requirements to attain this position, and our memorable journey through the multisite lean transformations began.

2

Cowboy Boots – *New Sheriffs in Town*

It was the start of many things: most notably a shift from the type of shoes we needed to wear. There were many expectations to set, and some sturdy boots were required to enforce them. To get started, the vision with values for our team needed to be established. We would hold ourselves accountable to them throughout our journey. Then there were the introductions: new people, new processes, and new ways of doing business. We had to build trust, respect, and a little faith in everything we were about to do. We would quickly learn about the importance of understanding one's current state and the value of transparency. We would also quickly enforce the importance of spending time on the floor as a team calibrating our views of what we were observing. All of these "new things" would set the foundation upon which we would build.

Setting the Vision

Kathy *Having won the shoot-out at the O.K. Corral and getting to name Shannon to the team, I was standing tall in my boots. The "new sheriff in town" had chosen one of her strategic deputies – one that was brave and could make things happen. I knew I had about 18 months before the senior executives would come to town and judge my ability to practice what I had been preaching for the past five years. More importantly, I genuinely believed in the power of lean principles to drive business performance. For me, it is a very personal badge of honor to run an organization*

DOI: 10.4324/9781003196976-2

with healthy manufacturing plants. I feel that most of the blessings in my adult life have been the result of creating factories that employ all types of people that are, in turn, able to support their families. For me, this leadership role was an opportunity to give back, and I did not want to waste any time waiting to implement the company's lean system that my former team had developed. I had to be strong in my conviction that this was the right way to run the business. There were so many forces working against this direction; sometimes the metrics themselves (like traditional cost accounting), the cultural norms and behaviors of your team, and the belief that, like other initiatives that had come and gone before, this would be yet another program of the month. If people just held out long enough, this too would meet its demise.

I consider myself a straightforward person. I had to communicate my leadership values and expectations for the team.

Values:

- *Current and Future State*
  - *Cannot overcommunicate*
  - *A shared vision of what good looks like*

- *Work as a team*
  - *No walls*
  - *No victim mentality*
  - *Trust and respect*

- *Work hard*
  - *Have fun*
  - *Work-life balance*

I repeatedly used this set of principles to reinforce my values and vision of a healthy team – the new ground rules. We had to accept the business's current state and create a future vision of growth and improved profitability. Consistent communication was a core value. I do not believe that you can overcommunicate with your team. In the absence of people hearing the truth from their leader, they will fill in the blanks with their interpretation of what is going on around them, most times not accurately. It was vital that we had a shared vision of the future, built on our strengths, and drove alignment throughout.

My direct reports were a team of leaders. They needed to grow as team leaders, but they also needed to be effective team members. We could discuss anything behind closed doors. I encouraged respectful debate, but when the discussion was over, and the direction had been determined, we left the conference room as a united front. I wanted to break down walls between engineering and manufacturing. I wanted everyone to understand what happened in the plant so that new products could be designed that had a chance of being successful in production.

Although empathy and active listening were two traits I worked desperately to excel at, I had no tolerance for a victim mentality and forbade finger-pointing among our team. Trust and respect were core values. I give trust freely – but if you lose my faith, it is tough to regain. I had been around the corporation and knew all the available expertise. I had to impress upon my new team that if I invited one of my friends from Corporate to help our team, there would be no defensiveness. We had nothing to hide and could truly benefit from those whose first line was always, "Hi, I'm __________. I'm from Corporate, and I'm here to help." By the same context, I needed my team to explain how we were unique, different, and special, and how the tools being shared with us could be adapted for maximum benefit.

Finally, we needed to work hard. I did not consider that a mutually exclusive concept from having fun. I believe in taking your job seriously, but yourself not so much. Work-life balance was an essential aspiration for me, and I would respect their pursuit of it as well.

As a "process person," I love to create structure and order where there was none before. One of my favorite words is "cadence." Rhythmic sequence, as in beautiful music, is what running a business feels like to me. I love the structure. Whether it's how I construct my daily calendar, how a product is built, or the order in which our roundtable discussion is conducted, that is the world in which I thrive. I needed my team to join me in that world.

As a "people person," I feel all should have the opportunity to contribute in a meaningful way. I also consider myself an optimist and can generate enthusiasm about what has and will be accomplished. Imagine the self-regulation I had to practice in the early days when my vision of the future was met with doubtful, yet polite, half-smiles and nods. My favorite moment was the blatant eye roll I got when I asked about how we scheduled the plant.

I was 90 days into this new job, and I was still recruiting a Controller and an Engineering Manager in the less than defined corporate hiring processes. Shannon had arrived, which was a big checkmark. My husband and I had closed on a house, another significant accomplishment (although we had not moved into it yet), and it was the summer between my daughter's high school graduation and first year of college.

With introductions behind me, it was time to make a bold statement about the new era we were embarking on together. Things needed to look and feel different. The first dramatic thing I did was to have the plant ceiling and walls cleaned and painted. That 1970s' paneling, which I had never been fond of (even when my parents proudly put it up in our family room during the short time of my childhood that it was actually in vogue), was painted white as well. It was time that the physical appearances of our facility reflected the excellence we strived to achieve.

I spent a lot of time on the shop floor making sure all the production status boards were up-to-date and consistent with the format and content that had been specified for the whole company. It was also time to enforce some basic housekeeping principles throughout the plant, establishing a place for everything and everything in its place. It was a way of creating an environment that was respectful to the people who spent most of their waking hours there.

When I had to do my first presentation of divisional performance results, I was a little nervous. I knew I would be asked what the $40k of facility expense was. There was no capital project associated with it. Every product group in the corporation had its personality. There was the serious group, the party group, the moral high-ground group, etc. The group I had found myself in was considered the frugal one, hence my anxiety. When the inevitable question arose, I took a deep breath and answered that it was for the E7P project. Everybody nodded as though they knew what the E7P project was – nobody dared show weakness or ask a question in this crowd. If it was worthy of a three-letter acronym, surely everyone should know what it was. I finished the rest of my slides with confidence. When I sat down next to the previous General Manager, whom I adored by the way (I called him Big Red), he leaned over and asked me what E7P was? I told him, "Eliminate 70s' Paneling." He laughed out loud. Not generally a risk-taker, more of a rule-follower, I had gotten away with it. Under normal circumstances, I would have asked permission and most likely been denied spending the money. I learned an important lesson that day: when in doubt, speak in three-letter acronyms. It helps you exude confidence.

Making cultural changes requires immense energy, genuine passion, and sometimes a big personality. Maybe people consider me to have one of those. I don't know. I do know that I am passionate about winning, including everyone on the team in the game, and having FUN while working hard. I am not the most traditional of leaders. I have different modes of operation that I can call upon when necessary, but "command and control" is not my primary style.

Leadership can be lonely. I was brought up in an environment where it was better not to be friends with your team members. Peers, okay, but direct reports needed to be kept at arm's length. This way, if you needed to drop the hammer, it could be done with minimal impact on your social life. So, when you are located in a place where peers are, at best, a phone call away, you do need someone with whom to commiserate. You need someone you can be 100% honest with without scaring those whom you lead. You need someone who has your best interest at heart, who owns your endeavors' success as much as you do. At least that is the operating model I had developed with my lean teacher, Rick Harris.

Getting Started

Rick and I had started working together in 2001. At that time, the company I was working for was all-in on lean, no "Plan B." They hired the people who had written the books. They dedicated resources, moved leaders aside that did not buy-in, and promoted those employees that "got it" and demonstrated a passion for it – people that could teach and inspire others – people that could truly transform how business is done. When I was promoted to run two of the large plants on one of the major campuses, Rick was assigned as my "sensei." Passionate about not being called an expert, he preferred the title "practitioner." He guided my team through a comprehensive transformation, culminating with being recognized as a Shingo Prize Recipient for Large Businesses. It was an excellent piece of acknowledgment for a team that was so smart and worked so hard. Every day, in a business with its financial struggles, it was like going to war, fighting costs, battling delivery, challenging past practices and the contract language, and sparring with senior executives under extreme pressure. Rick's guidance, confidence, and challenging demeanor were instrumental to the team's success. Rick and I made a pact to continue to work together whenever we had the opportunity to transform manufacturing plants into strong, viable, and competitive businesses. So, when I eventually left that company to be the lean leader at this company, Rick and I continued to work together in plants across the United States. And when that assignment had run its course, and I went to run this division, Rick was by my side.

As usual, he showed up and painted a picture of what the future would be if the team worked hard and followed his lead. The look of an overwhelmed team upon meeting Rick for the first time seriously never gets old. In every plant I had gone to, and I mean EVERY plant, there is a point within the first visit, usually in the first five minutes, when someone from the team (often the leader) makes a case for their business being different, unique and special. The implication is that this lean operating system does not apply to them. It was refreshing that my team did not actually voice this concern, even though I could see it in their faces. And I was just beaming as Rick spoke. I could hardly contain my excitement to show this company how a real lean transformation could be done under my leadership. Shannon will describe the "drinking from a fire hose" vibe of Rick's first visit below.

Shannon came down to divisional headquarters for Rick's first visit shortly after she joined the team. This was the site where I had my main office and housed one of our two largest plants. She stayed at a local hotel that she described as "unsettling." She told me she was sure it was haunted and needed to find somewhere else to stay for future visits. I invited her to stay with me. The house we had purchased was plenty big, and since I was part of the thrifty group, I figured it would save the company money. I never admitted to her (until she has read this chapter) that I was kind of nervous about staying in the house alone anyways. Anytime I could enjoy other human presence there, it was a bonus and guaranteed a good night's sleep. She was gracious in accepting my invitation and wanted to express her gratitude for providing a much more comfortable arrangement for her visits. She offered to bring her groceries and had some other suggestions to help out, but none of that was necessary from my perspective. After much persistence, I finally relented and told her that she could check the mail for me if she wanted to help out when she stayed. I once had an unfortunate mail-retrieving incident in which a family of spiders had decided to take up residence between the pieces of mail that had been shoved in there. I vowed never to check the mail again, so I truly appreciated her assistance. (I fully disclosed the incident to Shannon so that she could be adequately prepared for her new duty.)

As that first summer progressed, I started to settle into my new role. I hired a Controller and an Engineering Manager. I was getting used to the rhythm of the

30-day calendar cycle. There were the Tuesday morning results calls, the scorecard metric due dates, and the deep dives into the divisional numbers with my boss. We had kicked off the lean transformation, which was not an optional priority, and could pick the other strategic initiatives later in the year. It was a time of familiarization with my team, products, customers, the lake, and the new routine I had developed to make sure I could spend at least 50% of my free time with my daughters. I was blessed that my boss and my team were very supportive when I needed a flexible work location. I put what seems like millions of miles on straight country roads riding back and forth to be with my girls in those years. Summer was great, as they were able to spend most of the time at the lake with me.

During that first summer, an unfortunate incident occurred that had me pausing to reflect on a delicate topic that evoked mixed emotions in me. Throughout my career, I have rarely dwelt upon the fact that I am a woman in business. There were countless meetings where I was the only female. I was aware that conversations took place at urinals I would never be privy to and I didn't get invited to the golf leagues in which many of my peers participated. It was not an area of focus for me. I just wanted to do the best job I could wherever my career led me. Yes, there were countless examples of jokes I should not have heard, or questions about who was watching my children while I worked, or men who mistook gestures of friendship as an expression of attraction, but all along, those were just the hazards of the jobs I took and the career I had chosen. I was still able to be effective with what I was striving to accomplish. However, it was difficult to look the other way a couple of times when my gender put me at an authentic disadvantage in performing my job. And what took place that summer was a stark reminder that gender differences in the work world were still alive and well.

The General Manager job came with a country club membership. Although my husband is a golfer, we had never been members of any such establishment, and admittedly, we were a tad bit excited to have a place to socialize that had golf, tennis, and a fancy dining room. I believe this perk was established so that senior leaders could entertain customers with a round of golf or a nice meal and a cocktail. Not long after we had settled into our lake house, my husband suggested we check out our new club. We, along with my oldest daughter, Emily, headed that way. We opened the unlocked front door and called out to announce our presence. When nobody replied, we decided to explore. While we were checking out one of the rooms, one with dark wallpaper and an empty popcorn machine, a gentleman entered and asked if he could help us. I enthusiastically answered that we were new members and we were just taking a look around the club. He apologized that they were not yet open and uncomfortably shifted his weight back and forth as he looked at us, clearly searching his heart for what to do next. Following what seemed to be an eternity of awkward silence, I apologized and told him I had not thought it was a problem to walk around the building, as the front door was unlocked. He did confirm that it was, indeed, okay for us to be on a self-guided tour; however, my daughter and I had to leave the room we were currently in, as it was reserved for gentlemen only. "Excuse me?" I gasped. "This room is reserved for gentlemen only.

If the ladies would like a refreshment, there is a lemonade room on the other side of that wall." I have to say this was a bit shocking. I wondered if I would just have to sit in the adjacent room and pass notes back and forth via carrier pigeon to the men's refreshment area as I negotiated multi-million dollar deals with my customers. Emily stormed out of the room, through the front door, and went straight to our car. It was a few years and a revised policy on using that room to include both genders before she would return.

I wanted to think that in the early 2010s, this would have been the only place left in the civilized world that had such a policy. Unfortunately, I was acutely aware that our parent company also hosted work events at a club that only allowed men to golf. That was, of course, unless they wrote a special letter to get permission from the club, if heaven-forbid, a customer wanted to send a female golfer; or better yet, a woman were promoted to a position within the company that would obligate her to attend such an event. Luckily, I had only heard of that happening once. Every year, the employee opinion survey would have pages and pages of comments asking that customer events be hosted at a venue that did not exclude women. To my knowledge, when I left the company, those concerns had not yet been addressed.

It was unfortunate that Emily was along for the country club incident, as I had tried to shelter her from the realities of gender differences. I was attempting to be a role model as a working mom who wanted to excel in all realms of life. Emily was about to enter college, and I so wanted her to go on believing she could accomplish anything without prejudice or limitations.

While I wanted Emily to have those beliefs, I was emotionally struggling to let her go. In mid-July, we headed to college orientation, me a bundle of mixed emotions, mostly sad ones. Upon reaching campus, the orientation leaders immediately separated us into groups of parents and students. I don't know where they took Emily, but a nice lady in the parent group befriended me and engaged me in just enough small talk to keep me distracted. The parents were escorted into a large auditorium where they told us about privacy laws, that we would have no access to our children's progress or grades. They would, however, keep us completely in the know regarding the status of their bills, fees, and any other discretionary spending requirements our children would have. Things took a turn for the worse when they started to explain the different options for lunch plans. There were many to choose from, and the reality of her eating in a location so far from home just became too much to handle. I was no longer able to contain my tears. I was sure that I wasn't the only one, and I was well prepared with a purse full of extra-soft tissues. As I looked around to offer a tissue to any other parent that just could not be consoled, I did discover that I was, indeed, the only one visibly shaken by the meal plans. So, I continued to keep my head down and attempted not to make a scene. As soon as we left that tortuous presentation, my new friend immediately ditched me. The school eventually reunited us with our children. Emily was annoyingly excited with anticipation of embarking upon her college career. I somehow found the strength to hide my separation anxiety. Mission accomplished – the whole world of possibilities was opening to my little girl.

I think you are starting to get a picture of the environment that Shannon was entering when she came into my life. She immediately bonded with Emily, whom she gave emotional support when I would question Emily about what WE should bring to college. (I was always threatening to go back to school as her roommate, in a loving sort of way, of course.) And Claire, my youngest, and Shannon became fast friends when Claire told her about how "messed up" her family was due to the number of half and stepsiblings she had. Shannon's own family rivaled hers, and when the statistics were shared, Claire knew she had someone who got it, someone perfect to consult with regarding awkward family matters.

After a gut-wrenching scene of leaving Emily at college, I went back to work and tried hard to adjust to the new normal, which included an impending celebration trip for my staff and their spouses. My boss was a huge proponent that leadership teams that make their numbers should be rewarded. The planned trip consisted of a long weekend with a couple of business meetings but mostly recreation and fellowship (wineries, golfing, and meals) for the team. Any trip within driving distance was an available option. Before this experience, I hadn't realized the power of getting to spend time with a team in this way. It was so much fun and accelerated our bonding as a team. It was a way to show appreciation for all the spouses that put up with our extended hours, our sometimes silent evenings when we just didn't want to talk about our days, our frequent travels, and our moods. Who knew that these annual trips would be an important part of our team's story, trips where accomplishments were celebrated and legendary stories were born? We laughed so obnoxiously at one of the dinners on that first trip; I personally paid for the dinners of all the others around us at the restaurant who had looked forward to a lovely, relaxing evening out. These were the memories we created that made us more like a family than a band of colleagues as the years progressed.

Shannon was unsure if she should go on that first trip with us, as she would have to attend solo. Scott, her new husband, had a trip already planned and could not join us. I would not hear of her not participating. So, she did come. She went on the optional winery tour with Jeff and me, and well, another epic bonding story was born. I will let her tell you about that. I do remember her taking all kinds of guff from the team about a fake husband – one whose name she had not taken yet, one who had not shown up anywhere our group had gathered. Teasing is a form of affection in my family, so I left that first celebration weekend so happy. My cast of characters that had been assembled with the mission of creating the best business we could was becoming a real team.

Shannon

The lean job was finally mine, and I was ready to put my boots on and get to work. I'd held leadership roles in the past, but this was different. I would be helping to set strategy and direction – finally taking my seat at the leadership table. My first experience with the team was when we were introduced to Rick Harris. Kathy had brought Rick in to help guide us through our lean transformation, and his first visit to meet the team was mine as well. It was such an impactful but overwhelming day. I had an internal conversation with myself:

"Hi. I'm Shannon McCall. You've never met me, and I'm here to make you all do something you probably don't want to do." On a side note, Kathy mentioned that I had just gotten married but introduced myself with my maiden name. There were many questions around this, and I tried to explain that having been at that company for eight years, the connections I had made knew me by my maiden name. I'd had this name for 30-something years, so why should I have to be called something else?!? I was going through a bit of a comical identity crisis that Scott thankfully rolled with. I can only imagine what my new teammates were thinking about this crazy girl that wouldn't do something as basic as changing her name.

Anyway, I was still me. I knew we had a long way to go to reach the expectations. At that point, it all seemed so unachievable. I remember the executives in the room being very excited about the results we were going to achieve. However, the question on my mind was how to get us there, considering our plant's current state (sustainable processes lacking in my opinion). I wasn't the only one with this thought. You could tell that some of the team members were all-in. They were tired of working so hard and not seeing the improvement. Others were very skeptical and hoping this was another fad that would quickly go away. It was hard being in an influencing role with no direct authority and trying to get the skeptical team members on board. Even though I didn't know how we would get there, I believed in Kathy and Rick, and I knew that failure wasn't an option. In my mind, this is what we were going to do and how we were going to do it, and I believed it would work. I had implemented many of the tools in the past and had already been through one lean transformation. Although it was a different product line and type of manufacturing process, I knew it would work. The vision had been set, and I was not going to sway from that. It was difficult for me to work through the fact that others did not trust me immediately. They had been through many initiatives that previous leadership teams had pushed on them. I generally excel at taking ideas and turning them into action, but at that time, I did not genuinely understand the change cycle and how to help people through it. I was starting to realize that implementing the tools wasn't going to be the hard part. It was navigating through the team's varied emotions and prolific opinions that would end up taking most of my energy.

On that first day with Rick, Kathy asked me to be the note taker. She taught me the importance of taking very detailed notes, not only to capture what had been discussed but to document the entire journey – where we had come from and how we had gotten there. It's a good thing I am good at organizing because when Kathy said detailed, she meant detailed. Kathy will tell you that she likes things structured and a certain way, and I had to quickly adapt and accept feedback on how to change things without taking it personally. Since I am a bit of a perfectionist, I needed to figure that out in order to move forward quickly. I will admit that Kathy's way makes sense most of the time, and even if it doesn't, there's a reason behind it, so I learned to adapt.

From that first day forward, you would not catch me without a notebook, feverishly writing on any "Rick Harris Day." I wrote down everything, and I mean everything. Sometimes I wrote so fast that I couldn't read my terrible handwriting when I went back to read my notes. I would write questions he asked and the answers given. I scribed comments he made and ideas about future things to do. This is when Rick would look at me and say, "Don't do that yet, but write it down." I was not going to miss one piece of information that we discussed, not only for my own learning but to give the team the best shot at succeeding. I committed to making sure we had the homework documented. From the homework descriptions, action item lists were created. It was crucial to Kathy and me that we follow through on what we said we were going to do. There was no way I would disappoint Kathy or Rick by missing something. And let me tell you, this did happen a couple of times, and it did not feel good for the team or me. As a result, we implemented a review of the homework that Rick outlined to be completed before the next session before he left for the day. This turned out to be a powerful way to help the organization drive toward accountability. We were expected to report out on what we accomplished (or didn't) at the next visit, starting our journey on the Plan-Do-Check-Act (PDCA) cycle of accountability.

I published the notes and task lists for the homework and outlined the expectation that we should post these and assign owners with names and dates. Remember when I said I was learning that not everyone thinks like me? Well, I learned this the hard way after I sent out the task lists and came back a few weeks later to discover that the implementation team had not reviewed them, much less taken any action. This was when I learned the power of regular touchpoints and a weekly cadence for updates.

I also learned that task completion was much more successful when I would document high-level, significant actions, then work with the team to break them down into every single little thing that needed to be accomplished to get that one big item done. It helped me think through the process and for the team to learn that thought process. It also taught me to empathize with people who were already doing full-time jobs and getting assigned more work. We made these task lists very specific with each item being owned by the one person who had clear accountability for its completion by a certain date.

At times, I would get frustrated by people not getting their work done. I just couldn't understand this as we were given direction, and we just needed to do the work. I needed the team to care as much as I did and did not want our team to disappoint each other or our leaders with a lack of progress. I was learning that not everyone is motivated the same way. I had to figure out how to move the team forward. I started to realize that I needed to act differently now that I was a leader and not just an individual contributor. I decided to get more personally involved with each team member in their actions. "How can I help? Let's talk through it." I made a more concerted effort at being present and having those boots on the ground. Breaking down the tasks and getting to know the team started to move us in the right direction.

During this time, I started traveling to the headquarters a lot more often. This was challenging because I had just gotten married. However, Scott and I were committed to making this opportunity work. To maximize my time there, I decided to stay close to the plant, only to find out that there would be no sleep in the hotel I determined was haunted. (This is a story for another day!) Kathy and I were discussing this one evening at dinner at her kitchen table. As luck would have it, a giant bug appeared on one of her lake house walls. After seeing the look of terror on her face, I jumped up and killed it with the bottom of my shoe and a slight shriek. She immediately followed this gesture by handing me a key and welcoming me to stay there whenever I traveled to town. While she would have most likely given me a key either way, due to her all-inclusive nature and needing me to actually get some sleep to get the amount of work done that was requried, I think that giant bug helped seal the deal.

If you have traveled much, you will understand how amazing it was to have an actual house to stay at, with a kitchen to cook real food in, and a place to keep essentials instead of repacking them every week. I bought groceries to cook at the house instead of eating out every night. This became a quick ritual where I would try to come up with something healthy to throw together for us. Kathy was so grateful that she wouldn't have to eat cereal or microwave popcorn for dinner on the nights I was there. (Please note that neither Kathy nor I excelled at cooking at this phase in our lives, so this was a bit of an experience.) We worked long hours, so on the nights we were both there, it was nice to rehash our days and laugh over something decent to eat with a glass (or bottle) of wine. And so our trust in each other and bond started to grow.

Understanding Current State

Back at the plants, my first mission was to understand the current state. What were the processes? Who were the people? How were we performing? I have to say my first walk through the plants was disappointing. There was no order that I could readily identify. It was dirty and dark, and I thought, if only I was able to help with some cleanup and organizing, that would be a win – not to mention my shoes and rolled-up pant hems were getting dirty! Kathy and I are both very structured people that value organization and processes that don't fall apart if one person is out for a day. We had work to do to create this world.

We quickly agreed that we did not have a way to know if we were winning day to day or the ability to see normal from abnormal. There were many other questions that we couldn't answer: What told us that we won or lost yesterday? Where were our issues documented? Were there systemic issues we didn't recognize because we were so good at reacting and fixing? Were we going to make customer commitments today? In manufacturing, every day counts. Misses add up and cause us to disappoint our customers.

Although there was a standard set of visual boards specified in the company's lean system, the discipline to keep them up had somehow lapsed somewhere along the way. They needed to be implemented again, sustainably this time. We started with a "Daily Run-the-Business" Meeting, facilitated by a plant-level board that displayed key metrics. It had included productivity, quality, safety, and delivery metrics for each value stream in the plant.

The intent was an update, not an in-depth problem-solving session. We conducted the meeting in the plant, so all the team members knew how we had performed the day before. We quickly realized it was difficult to hear, so we acquired a microphone, and the era of using a microphone was born at every plant walk, tour, and discussion going forward. This in itself was a culture change. Everyone had to speak to their numbers and be heard, with accountability being driven by site leadership.

It wasn't quite as simple as it sounds. It took a while for all the team members to understand that attendance wasn't optional. It took time for the team to get into the rhythm of this process. Consistency was key. Kathy would attend these meetings initially and hold the team members accountable for attendance, ownership, and action. Her setting the expectations and not wavering from them drove stability into the process.

As this board and its accompanying daily meeting became institutionalized, it started to drive teamwork across the plant. The accountability was not only on the Manufacturing Managers but equally with the support departments. If engineering or quality support was needed, it was being requested at the meeting. The support teams were rising to the occasion, and trusting relationships started to blossom.

The next level of boards that needed to be implemented again were the Value Stream Tracking Centers. These were the boards that displayed current and future states of the value streams being transformed in the plant, as well as the high-level and detailed action plans that would facilitate future states with significantly less waste and consequently reduced lead times – which were the amount of time it took products to flow through our facilities to our customers. These were also located in the plant and where the improvement meetings were held by the cross-functional team performing the work. Making them visible and inclusive left no question as to what changes were being made and the expected impact. They drove the Plan-Do-Check-Act (PDCA) cycle in the transformation process.

The final level of boards were team improvement boards. These boards were set up to help high-performance teams within the value streams to improve their work area. They consisted of safety, quality, delivery, and productivity metrics that were chosen by the team as meaningful to drive performance. This is where structured problem-solving meetings among team members eventually took place. The metrics on these boards contributed to the key metrics that were tracked for the plant but were different. For instance, at the plant-level board, we measured productivity as sales/employee and wages/sales. People running the machines really had nothing to do with sales, so they measured pieces/hour produced. At first, the boards were just put in place to hold the daily start of shift team meetings. It would be a while for the entire population to participate in the problem-solving efforts.

Gemba Walks – Go and See

With the introduction of the metrics and boards to track them, we started daily group Gemba walks as a leadership team. Gemba is a Japanese term for "the actual place" or the place where value is created. For us, this was in the factory or "on the floor," as many call it. These walks were put in place for a number of reasons – the first of which was to have the leadership team be visible throughout the operation on a consistent basis. The second was to calibrate the leadership team on Kathy's expectations of manufacturing discipline. The third was to identify areas of improvements and make sure the ones previously made had been sustained.

The walks consisted of a 5S observation followed by a process observation. The 5Ss stand for Sort, Straighten, Shine, Standardize, and Sustain. 5S is a system for organizing areas so that people can work safely and efficiently with only the items needed to do the work. It is fundamental in setting the foundation for everything on which the lean system is built. 5S is a powerful tool that leads to improved productivity, a safer work environment, and facilitating your ability to identify abnormal conditions. In the beginning, there was a lot of work to do to improve our level of 5S, which is why it was essential to include it in our daily Gemba walks.

At first, even short walks would generate long lists of items that needed to be improved. However, over time, we would limit action items left in an area to no more than three, so as not to overwhelm the teams. Any safety hazard had to be immediately addressed. Not always did the area owner have all the assignments. Sometimes, it required maintenance, engineering, or quality to resolve issues.

Over time, the findings began to transform through each "S" from: "what is this stuff?" to "where does this stuff go?" to "why is that stuff out of place?" to "what can we do to make this stuff more efficient for the operator?" It's powerful to watch the progression the team takes through this journey by learning to observe. A great way to document the progress is to use a structured 5S audit to measure each team. Rick Harris also taught us to look through our customers' eyes. Would they trust us with new business if we couldn't manage a clean, orderly house? How much confidence could we build with our customers if they walked the plant and saw everything in its place? It was a new perspective for many. Everyone on the floor saw how important this was to Kathy and the leadership team, which made adopting the principles a little bit easier, especially as time went on and this process was consistently followed.

The process observations followed the same cycle, but these observations were a little looser in structure. We would do a standard work audit if standard work was available. (Early in our journey, we did not have standard work established for all processes; however, this did become the requirement as we progressed.) Sometimes we would just make basic observations of the process. Rick had taught us the ground rules around making effective observations. They always started with showing respect to the operators by explaining what we were doing and why. He also taught us not to talk while doing observations, so that we could truly concentrate on what we were observing. Rick would say, "It's difficult to observe while you are talking." This practice was new to us and not as easy as it seems. As a culture, we are not comfortable with silence and found ourselves invariably whispering to each other. We would spend about 5–10 minutes in observation, document our notes, and share/ask questions at the end of the observation. What was so crucial to this process was the sustainment factor. Once we put a new process in place, we would observe it as a team once a week to ensure it worked the way we had intended during its design. We would diagnose why it may not have sustained itself or, if it had, what further improvements could be made. There is a lot of power in doing this as a team. Not only will everyone know every process in the plant, but we learned from each other how to see and how to problem-solve when something wasn't working quite right because, let's be real, not everything works exactly the way we thought it would.

Kathy

"Gemba walks" are an activity I feel strongly about. I had learned from my previous experience that you must spend time on the floor daily. I used the walks as a way to check that the gains made were being sustained. I also used them as a way to teach my leadership team to see what I saw as we went through the factory. When I say my leadership team, I mean my whole leadership team, not just those running manufacturing. It was important for engineering to see how product design impacted yield, how processes had to be modified, or how the product had to be reworked due to the capability of the equipment. Marketing could use the plant as a selling tool (eventually) and Human Resources could help with attendance or morale issues, to give a few examples.

These walks were held in what I labeled "sacred" timeslots. That meant that they were to be given priority for attendance and nobody, but nobody was to schedule other meetings during that timeslot. That included me. We had to give the factory time to understand yesterday, prioritize today, make continuous improvements, and sustain the gains we had made the day before and the day before that. We had to show up, so the people running the equipment knew we respected them; we were there for them consistently. I even preferred that they knew when we were going to show up. They knew it would only be 24 hours to have access to the entire leadership team. I made it a priority to show up consistently as the routine was being established. I said that I would be there, barring an incident like the ceiling falling (which did happen to me once during an earlier part of my career). Over time, when I believed the team had truly understood the value of this process, I backed off my attendance a bit. I trusted the team to run their operation, and when I showed up, I found everyone talking and focusing on me. It was not about me. It was about them.

Shannon

The level of conversation began to change and elevate as we continued to follow this PDCA structure. The structure itself was important because it gave the team the confidence to know what to expect each day and each team member's role in it. As mentioned earlier, it also fostered a supportive environment. Kathy was very passionate about allowing the team to build confidence in each other and knowing that they could count on their teammates. It facilitated those common and achievable goals toward the same overall objective. We were not just transforming the manufacturing space, but we were also building a strong culture of inclusivity. By creating clear roles where each person had their respective level of accountability, each person's voice was heard. It was only the beginning.

During this early cadence development, data mining, team formation, and current state assessment, Kathy was arranging a trip for the leadership team to celebrate the previous year's performance and create the next year's strategy. I was very hesitant to join since I was new to the team, and my new husband couldn't come due to previous commitments. Kathy was so welcoming and convincing (both strengths of hers) that I reluctantly agreed to participate. I packed up for what I imagined was to be a solo and highly uncomfortable weekend. But after a day of wine tasting with Kathy and her husband (and a memorable parking lot beverage concocting which he called a "booster"), my bond with them was pretty much solidified. I looked up to them both and developed a connection that I greatly valued – not to mention how much we laughed.

My relationship with the team evolved that way too. I was the youngest and least experienced member of the leadership team, but after being teased about my fake husband (again, no name change, and he wasn't there), I had a feeling that I belonged. I will forever be thankful that Kathy convinced me to go on that trip to the lodge, not only for the bonding that took place but because for the first time in my career, I was able to be a part of setting the strategy as a valued member of the leadership team. It is one thing to implement a vision that is "handed down" to you – it is another to be part of its creation.

It was time to change our shoes once again. We set our cowboy boots aside and laced up our steel toes – time to get to work on the shop floor.

3

Steel Toes – *Time to Hit the Plant Floor*

These were still early days and crazy, busy times. While we were focusing on work, life was going on around us. Life is not too worried about your lean transformation, your Tuesday calls, your professional development. Nor does your work slow down to accommodate what is going on in your personal life. It's our job to balance both, to the extent with which each of us is personally comfortable. And the inputs keep coming from all directions. Some give us energy, and some suck the life out of us.

We worked together to weed through these inputs and determine what was essential and what to ignore. It was challenging to do so, but it was all part of having a new team planning significant business changes. We had to begin to learn how to work together to prioritize the needs of our business and support each other. This would require a lot of coaching and providing feedback at every level in the organization.

We needed to start prioritizing our calendars with some serious time outside of conference rooms and in the plants. To do this, Rick suggested that our transformation team divide into three. One team would build a Plan For Every Part (PFEP) with every detail about every part to calculate required inventory levels, warehouse space, and much more. Another team would create standard work, understand capacity by creating operator and machine balance charts, and determine the strategy for which parts would run on which machines. The last team focused on material movement. This team would design tugger routes (a.k.a material delivery

DOI: 10.4324/9781003196976-3

routes), determine container strategies, and decide how the parts would be presented to the operators to maximize their productivity safely.

This would require some significant time in our steel toes, observing and collecting a lot of data. We needed to drive a sense of urgency to get moving at a pace some were uncomfortable with and, at times, required resources that were not readily available. We would have to utilize our team members' strengths and get creative with how we would get all this work done.

Feedback

Kathy

Have you ever been told that feedback is a gift? I hate when people say that. Whenever I have to take 360 surveys or have my performance appraisal, I get a nervous knot in my stomach. Every one of them is geared toward providing feedback on where you need to improve. They never are just "what I like about you." I am a perfectionist. And even though I vehemently deny it, I would like it if everyone liked me. You have to do difficult things in leadership that people may not completely understand, making you unpopular with the masses at times. However, I don't particularly appreciate that those in my "circle of trust," such as my boss, peers, and direct reports, are asked to provide developmental feedback. I know "that which doesn't kill you makes you stronger." I use the phrase often. But I am a firm believer in positive feedback. Let's have everybody focus on their strengths and do more of them.

On the other hand, I do not believe in false flattery or being dishonest either. We all have developmental needs. Having open, honest conversations about them is important, especially if you can coach someone to draw on the positive aspects of their skills and behaviors as resolution. And I certainly don't believe in hiding your honest feedback behind a cloak of secrecy in an anonymous survey. If you don't have the courage to have a conversation with someone about their blind spots, you probably don't care enough about them that your opinion should matter that much anyway. You most certainly don't belong in a position of leadership.

I was also well aware that my team needed a lot of positive feedback and coaching. Our lean transformation was unchartered territory, especially the material movement shift we were trying to make. It is a dramatic and painful change to take people who used fork trucks as personal industrial vehicles to move throughout a plant – with empty forks and put them on routes in which they are delivering material over 90% of the time. The feedback I have received repeatedly is that people would generally rather give up their firstborn child than get out of a seat in a fork truck. People aspire to these types of jobs – its rewards are many, particularly attaining the freedom of not being tied to a production line and being able to get to lunch much more quickly than their colleagues on foot. However, every implementation of lean that I had done thus far required us to limit fork truck traffic to the warehouses and put the drivers on vehicles that tug material through the plant on a regular schedule. The tugger drivers would deliver parts as the people in manufacturing needed them and remove empty used containers simultaneously. This became the most critical job in the plant, as it was the leadoff operation for all production. This transition for a fork truck driver is like going from the kid who used to sit in the very back of the classroom and did assignments as the spirit moved him to move to the front row and become the teacher's most valued helper. Fork truck drivers value the loose connection to the plant's rhythm, not the rigor of working 50 out of 60 minutes each hour and everybody depending on them to meet their productivity goals. So, I was all over positive feedback as we transitioned to this method of delivering material in the plant. When we started to implement routes, I would clear my calendar and follow the route with the tugger driver all day. When asked if I didn't have anything better to do, I would provide the feedback that no, this was the most critical part of my job on said day. It was all about positive reinforcement for the drivers and the team helping make this transition.

I also knew that this was a time when Shannon would need a lot of positive feedback. Her predisposition is to do what is asked of her and expects the same of those she is leading or influencing. People don't always respond that way. She could get frustrated easily, as she had always been a high achiever, and people getting in the way of achieving her goals was a new experience for her. I spent a lot of time reinforcing that she was doing the right thing and coaching in different ways to motivate people. I also knew that there were times she would feel lonely as a member of the new regime shaking up the time-honored ways of doing things. I wanted her to succeed. I owed her the time and energy to cheer her on, but sometimes a bit of tough love was in order too. She didn't always love the feedback, but she would generally come back after some time to process and offer appreciation for the spirit in which it was offered. She knew I was her biggest fan.

Sometimes, feedback does not have to be heavy and emotional. When someone is blowing off steam and needs to be heard about something, a reminder to keep a big bottle of ibuprofen around at all times would be utterly appropriate feedback. It is a critical piece of personal protective equipment needed in operations, and sometimes that reminder is needed. This particular line of feedback was offered in the spirit of, "I feel your pain. I have been there. Now shake it off and get back out there!" If I haven't mentioned it yet, let me say it right now: a manufacturing career is not for the faint of heart.

Shannon

I, too, have been told many times that feedback is a gift. While I believe in some cases this can be true, if not given appropriately, it can also be destructive. This was when giving and receiving feedback at every level in the organization needed to be handled delicately. We were asking the team to modify the way they were thinking and change almost every way they had done their jobs to that point. This was often frustrating and sometimes resulted in less than positive reactions. We wanted to ensure we were creating an environment for healthy debate and voices to be heard, but we also needed to make sure these discussions were productive. There were countless conversations I found myself in that required extreme patience. I was coaching others on how to address their concerns in a more positive, less frustrating way.

I was learning to provide this feedback while at the same time needing a lot of my own. I was often just as frustrated about the prevalent negative attitudes initially and the lack of execution that occurred at times. I thrived when, even at points of frustration, Kathy would coach me on approaching situations, giving examples of how she had witnessed me displaying appropriate reactions in the past. She knew what I needed, and it was not a lot of criticism that I had already given myself in my head. There were times that she told me to toughen up and not worry about people who were not getting on board, and that was also helpful because it was constructive, and I ultimately knew she believed in me and wanted me to be just as successful as I wanted to be. (And occasionally she let me borrow a couple of ibuprofen tablets she had stashed in an industrial size bottle under her desk!)

This is the sign of a good leader – one that takes the time and cares enough to get to know you and tailors the feedback in a way to help you grow. This is the type of leader I wanted to be. I would get the opportunity to practice this approach many times during this transformation because, in all honesty, yes, implementing the tools can be difficult, but changing people's hearts and minds is significantly more challenging.

We will always receive feedback, the good, the bad, the unwelcome, the unsolicited, and we have a choice on how we want to handle it. We can discard it, dwell on it, accept it, apply it. Just remember that sometimes things worth doing are hard. I have learned to give myself a little bit of space, sometimes having to grieve outcomes I would not have preferred. Feedback is no different than that little voice in your head – sometimes it is helpful, and sometimes it is not. "Please put on your steel toes and get back out there!"

Material and Information Flow

Continuing down our path of understanding the current state of our information, material, and people flows, there was a significant shift in thinking that we had to deploy. That was the separation of Production Control and Manufacturing. Supervisors were running around with "Hot Lists," rearranging parts to build/ship specific orders every day. They would get these lists from Customer Service, and the level of "hotness" was determined by who was yelling the loudest. The funniest part (maybe not to those who were deep in this process, trying very hard to satisfy the customer, but to outsiders) was when we uncovered that there were varying levels of Hot. There was: Hot, Super Hot, Super Hot in Red Ink, and Flaming Hot. OK, maybe not ALL of those levels were specified, but you get the point. (You really can't make this stuff up). How can you satisfy your customers when you are robbing Peter to pay Paul every single day? Jumping one order over the next? You can't. There was no flow, and production could not make everything needed on time. In reality, no one was satisfied, not to mention the sheer number of boxes full of parts all over the plant floor. So, we started to learn the difference in the roles between Production Control and Operations. Basically, Production Control makes the plan, Operations executes the plan. Production Control decides what to make based on customer demand/info and becomes the communication point from Customer Service. This separation allows operations to safely make as many good parts as possible every hour, every day. The Operations team does not need to know what is due when, only what part is running and which one is running next. And, the only reason needed to know what is running next is to prepare setups for that part.

Imagine the progress you can make and the time saved by not having supervisors running around the plant all day chasing orders! When describing this, it sounds easy, define the roles and go with it, but it was a much larger cultural change than I could have imagined. This was how the team had done it for years and years and with so many partially made products on the floor everywhere, how could the operators possibly know what to make next? The answer is, they couldn't.

So now what? We had to get through all of that work-in-process (WIP) inventory to control the material's flow. We made a conscious decision to put extra hours and labor to process these partially made orders of parts until we had reached a controllable level to move forward. It took weeks to do this, and to be completely transparent, it did not stick after the first cleanup.

We would walk the floor and find those famous hotlists hiding in multiple locations. We did our best to remove them when we found them. Many carried them in their back pockets. And just in case you are wondering, we did stop short of frisking all the supervisors! It took multiple iterations of applying additional labor and overtime to become stable. We were adding costs to the business that really could have been avoided; however, it was necessary to go backward to get to a point where we could go forward. Let me tell you how frustrating it was to keep finding those lists and see that these "clean-ups" seemed to be going to waste, only to find ourselves back where we started. It truly is all part of the learning process. We questioned ourselves about how we were going to sustain this and flow the product. As Rick Harris said to us one day, "When we can control processes, we can control inventory." And that is where the first team comes in.

The "Plan for Every Part Team" (PFEP): this team had a daunting task. They had to collect data on every single part number produced and create a tool (we used a spreadsheet) to store it in. So where do you begin when you have 10,000's of part numbers? You have to break it down to a much more manageable level. We started by choosing a value stream where our efforts would significantly impact our business performance measurements. A value stream is not a process department. It is a series of processes that run through the plant, that when done sequentially, produce a finished product from the raw materials delivered to the plant. We started with one such value stream to turn it into a model, so the other parts of the plant could learn what the future would look like in terms of processes and flowing value, not to mention the improved performance that the team would get. We chose a value stream that did not have large variances in cycle times, neither the easiest nor the most difficult. Since this PFEP tool was going to be used for multiple purposes, there were many data points to be collected, especially when you break down the three main inventory types: Purchased/Raw, WIP, and Finished Goods. We started with purchased parts because we needed consistent supplier deliveries and correct inventory levels to manage flow through the plant and handle customer demand swings. This was part of our efforts to stabilize the factory. If you don't have material available when you need it, where you need it, flowing value to the customer is much more challenging to achieve.

There are approximately 20 pieces of data that need to be entered into the PFEP for every part number in the plant. To size the purchased parts market, you need box quantities the supplier ships in, box dimensions, the weight of the part and box, etc. Many times, this information is not loaded into an ERP (Enterprise Resource Planning) system or documented anywhere, for that matter, so manual weighing and measuring is required. This request was baffling to the team. "You want us to go out and measure and weigh every box?" "Yes, yes, we do." (Please note there are times in this journey when you truly don't have enough people to do this type of work, so think about utilizing the help of summer students, interns, temporary employees, etc. to accelerate data collection). The vision is to develop a market (aka shelving or racking) where you can go to an address and find a part number every single time. In that market, parts are stored in the correct dimensions, by height primarily, to reduce air storage. Often the box quantities and sizes weren't standardized, and the supplier would ship in whatever box was available, in various amounts, to satisfy the purchase order. The purchasing team would have to work with the suppliers to standardize what we wanted to be delivered every time. To determine the number of parts to be stored in the market, data such as average daily usage, supplier lead times, supplier delivery performance, and scrap factors were used. This data collection allowed us to understand our suppliers' impact on how much inventory we needed to hold and how much space we needed. All of this information would continue to grow, be better understood, and be used in many different ways to help control production.

While the PFEP Team (and friends) measured boxes, the Materials Team started on their quest to determine how the material would flow through the plant. One of the first questions to be answered was, how do you know where anything is in the building? Whether it was machines or material, we didn't have a way to do this without saying it's machine XYZ and everyone knows it's over there (insert eye-rolling). Ok, but what if there is an emergency? The first responders wouldn't know where machine XYZ was. So, to continue on the mission of shifting the business to process orientation and not a "tribal knowledge" culture, which depended on the knowledge of the workforce, we created a master address system using the structural columns. We painted the individual address on each of them. Now everyone knew where they were if they just looked up. And all locations of parts and machines could be located with certainty by anyone. We usually don't recommend a lot of permanent paint for lean transformations, as we want to make layouts easier to rearrange as we continue to learn and improve. However, the structural columns in a manufacturing plant are not going to change, so they are a good anchoring point to guide people and material flow. We invited the local emergency responders into the plant and explained our new system -- they considered it a significant improvement should an accident occur. We were proud that this simple master address system had simplified our communication and improved safety at the same time!

Rick then challenged the Materials Team to develop a container philosophy. I remember thinking, "Is this a thing? How could I have ever predicted I would be philosophizing on what kind of box/tote to put parts in?!?" I felt the same way when I started to care about steel commodity prices too, but alas, here we were. It is a real thing and an important one at the start of figuring out how the material will flow. What container size makes sense? Should it be covered to protect the parts from dust and debris? How many container sizes should be allowed for a part? How many sizes should be allowed in the plant overall? A myriad of questions had to be answered. This is where some trial and error and getting on a first-name basis with your local plastic container person comes in very handy.

There is also setting the vision on HOW parts were going to move. At this particular point in time, the operators left their machines to get their parts and take their finished parts to the next process. How could they possibly be productive and maintain quality when they were leaving their machines to walk around? We also had supervisors and group leaders chasing down material with yet another form of "hot list" to bring to the operators. And what would happen if the group leader didn't get there in time? The operator might just stand there and wait. They might check their phone, work on 21 down on their crossword puzzle, or partake in other forms of entertainment that helped pass the time and made Kathy crazy. Productivity was everywhere to be had if we could just figure this out.

If we didn't want the operators or leaders getting the material, who would get the material and how would they know what to bring? That's where the future vision of information flow and material delivery came in. What type of equipment should you use and who would deliver it? Again, more trial and error and design concepts for your process/manufacturing engineers to work through. We also realized that we needed to create a new position to run the material delivery routes, as traditional fork truck drivers with their historic practices were not ideal candidates. With that, we learned (or maybe we were told, but quickly agreed) that this was the most critical position in the plant and, therefore, would require a pay increase. If you didn't have material where it needed to be when it needed to be there, most of the other endeavors were inconsequential. We started by appointing a person to be the only material handler for the plant to pick up everything via a 2-tiered pushcart. It was a very clunky process at first. Our "driver" manually created his list of which machines needed what materials. At one point, he had totes stacked so high he could barely see where he was pushing! He did this so he wouldn't have to make multiple trips. We asked him to take the productivity hit and make as many trips as needed to be done safely. He was the one figuring out how to be efficient. Since he was becoming intimately involved in the process, he gave us the most ideas on the best way to deliver the material. Involve and empower those closest to the work, and you will go much faster.

Another critical success factor was once the route was established, every leader in the plant had to run it. Now, I am not allowed to operate moving equipment. This is a self-induced rule based on my lack of confidence in my machine-operating skills. This rule also applies to power tools. So, I walked the route and did the work without doing the driving. The point is that we all knew how it worked and could see gaps in the system in real time, not how it would have been typically designed to work in a conference room. We were trying to change the culture at the same time as we were implementing all of these processes. Having our team members see that you care enough to want to perform their job and understand their struggles through experience was a game-changer. As a result of this iterative process, we ended up with a motorized tugger that pulled carts and the material handler could get on and off quickly to pick up and deliver containers at each stop, labeled with the master address for that stop.

It took many months to get the tugger and carts into operation for various reasons; learning that we needed quad steering on some carts to get around tight corners, getting the shelving heights correct, and other such items. The most significant delay, however, was when the orange tugger carts finally arrived. Why would this be a delay, you might ask? Well, this is how it went: I sent Kathy an email entitled "Carts are here!!" with a picture attached (clearly excited since we'd waited months for them to arrive). Kathy: "I pictured them in yellow." I replied: "We ordered them in yellow, but they came in orange." Kathy: "They need to be sent back at their expense and come back yellow." Apparently, Kathy hates the color orange.

Kathy

In all fairness, hate is a strong word. Orange is ok when it comes to fruits and vegetables, but not tugger carts, especially when ordered in YELLOW. Yellow was the color we had chosen as part of our 5S standards for our material movement, so people would be accustomed to looking for it. They needed to go back.

Shannon

Following this email discourse, there was an in-person discussion with me saying this was ridiculous. We could start getting the productivity now (something we were regularly reminded of by upper management that we were not yet achieving), and who cares about the damn color anyway!?! And quite honestly, I may have even stomped my cute high-heeled black pumps while saying this.

Kathy *I did not appreciate her stomping her feet in my office, mainly because I did not want her to damage the cute shoes I may want to borrow at some point!*

Shannon Kathy held her position, and I needed to tell the team they had to send them back. We quickly got over our disagreement on the carts, and they were returned in a fabulous, safe, bright yellow.

Kathy *And we all lived happily ever after!*

Balancing People and Machines

Shannon Simultaneous to the cart debacle, the third team worked diligently on understanding the current state of the production machines and people. The Manufacturing Team was collecting cycle times, uptime, and changeover times, to name a few of the data points, to understand each machine's capacity. We took the same approach, starting small, focusing on a couple of machines at a time within our model value stream. We were also learning what the operators already knew and what the best changeover sequence was through the data collection and observations. Rick would remind us that we needed to know as much as the operators did. We needed to gain their trust and ask for reasonable improvements, and the best way to do that was to truly understand what each operator was required to do for every operation in the plant.

Many hours were spent observing and documenting the steps that operators were using to make the products. This was the start of creating standard work. Standard work documents consist of content, sequence, timing, and outcome. Without these four key elements, listing the steps in order is merely a work instruction. We need to know crucial steps, in which order, how long each step takes, and the overall time to complete a process to set the standard to which the process is measured. The outcome portion of the standard work should also include how many pieces per hour the process should output so the machines' goals can be set and measured. Writing standard work is not a quick process, nor should it be. It should be done carefully with accurate math and operator input. It should be constantly reviewed and continuously improved. Since we were just starting, it was about getting the standard work documented and tracked.

Each piece of equipment should have a measurement tool to track actual output versus the goal determined by the standard work. We used a day-by-hour chart to track the pieces per hour targets. The chart would consist of a target number of pieces for each hour required to be completed from the standard work, and the operators would record what they had actually produced. This enabled them to know if they had a successful day or not. It also allowed for the supervisors to know if the customer commitments would be met each hour. If the goals were not met, it gave them time to make decisions immediately versus waiting until the end of the day when the reaction time to recover was too late. The charts had space for the operator to log why a target was missed and a supervisor sign-off section to review and acknowledge the miss. Reasons for misses were rolled up to the Team Improvement Boards at the end of the shift to do problem-solving to reduce recurring issues.

There are different philosophies on how to go about implementing standard work and day-by-hour charts. You could implement standard work first to set a reasonable target or put up day-by-hour charts and have the operators start tracking with no target or an average based on past performance (for example). I was planning to take the traditional approach of writing the standard work, take out waste where you could, then track to that goal with day-by-hour charts. Kathy had an alternative approach that quite possibly led to our largest disagreement to date. Kathy's experience had told her that you get 20% productivity gain just by measuring processes. I was thinking about the backlash we would receive about unreasonable goals and what it would do to morale. As we were arguing and glaring at each other across the conference room table, I believe it ended with me saying "fine" and putting the boards out there. And I admit she was right. And I was too. Operators were frustrated with some of the goals, but we did get them corrected over time, and it did help set a baseline by tracking the data early on. Oh, and we did get that immediate productivity gain. So, this is my way of saying I guess she was right (insert eye-rolling again) and quite possibly, I've made many of my teams since then do the same thing (insert giggling). We went quite a few days after that, not speaking, and I remember saying, "You can't be mad at me because I'm mad at you. That is not how it works!" followed by laughing on both sides. I bring this up because there will always be disagreements and differences in opinions on how things are done, but if everyone has a common goal, it doesn't need to be contentious or unpleasant. For us, it was a mere blip that we now laugh about and acknowledge that it only made our relationship stronger. Going through these storming phases of building teams that Kathy referred to is all a part of the process.

It was an interesting point in the transformation because in one plant, the operators welcomed the goals to know if it was a good day or not, and in another plant, the operators were outraged that they had to show how they performed each hour. We spent a lot of time talking to the operators explaining the intent. It was not about blame if a goal was missed. It was to identify issues and help us get better. Over time and continual communication, this would become part of everyone's daily routine. Not all operators would embrace it, but it is a required part of the process. To get the engagement, it is crucial to take the notes being documented on the day-by-hour boards and work to solve some of the recurring issues. If you don't do this step, it will become another "check the box" type of tool, and operators will begin to question why they even bother spending their time writing comments down. It's like that report your boss asks you to do every week that you never receive questions or comments on, and you wonder what the point is for this task. (You know what I'm talking about).

Once the machine data was collected, we dedicated parts to machines to fully understand each machine's capacity. We also needed to do this to size the cycle stock or "run quantities" for each part. Running the same amount of parts every time you run that part (Every Part Every Interval – EPEI) allows you to standardize what quantity comes off the machine and how often in order to standardize container size and pick up/delivery frequency. See how this is all tied together? This data also is input to building finished goods markets. These markets help to buffer against demand fluctuations from the customer by having a specified amount of material completed, determined by math.

Lastly, the Manufacturing Team was working on understanding what the people were doing. These observations and data collection would be built into operator balance charts and identify where we had extra wait time. It also helped us see how we could utilize the people better. We found out we could get more pieces per person when one operator ran two or more machines, but less per machine. This balance of people and machines is a tricky one, but as your understanding deepens, more improvements are identified as you progress.

There are so many details and so much data collection that goes into these steps. It is hard work that takes commitment from the whole team to drive this type of transformation. It is not for the weak at heart, that's for sure. It is entirely possible to do, but it takes coaching, trial and error, and a whole lot of patience to get it done. (I promise it's worth it!) "We are putting together a system – there are all pieces of the puzzle, and then all we have to do is handle exceptions," Rick Harris.

Communication Is Key

Communication is another huge piece of the puzzle. There is no such thing as over-communicating. While we were doing a decent job with one-on-one and small group communication, we needed to get a broader, universal message out. To do so, we started doing monthly plant communication meetings to give updates on the improvements we'd been making. Simply sharing the performance of the division and the individual plants from the previous month went such a long way in helping people feel connected. They started to understand that their jobs made a difference. They also began to understand how the business' success was being measured and how they fit in. Transparency and consistent messaging about the goals were vital.

These processes and puzzle pieces required steel toes on the ground (you choose the style), talking to the people closest to the work, building trust in the organization, and the occasional sheriff to keep things straight. As we continued to walk through and understand our current state, we realized that we needed to do a lot of training for our people to help them be more engaged and effective. We had a great group of people; however, they had not been exposed to what good looks like, so we added training shoes to our wardrobe and got to work!

4

Training Shoes – *So Much Training, So Little Time*

Although the vision and values had been well established, we needed to have a comprehensive strategy to align all resources to the key priorities. It is not an easy task deciding on the critical few things that would have the largest impact on the business, but the team was up to the challenge. Once the priorities were established, a lot of training was required to bring the team up to speed on the new tools and processes we would be putting in place. Alongside these changes, there were a number of operational basics that did not measure up to standards – safety practices among them. These all needed to be addressed sooner rather than later.

Creating the Strategy

Kathy *Shannon and I both mentioned the trip we took with the spouses/significant others (or, in Shannon's case, sans spouse or figment of her imagination)*

Shannon Very funny!

Kathy *And how it took the team to new levels of performance. And as I mentioned, I fantasized about going from forming to norming and skipping the storming stage. However, you cannot avoid the step of storming. It is required to go through so that norming can be aligned and productive. Storming neither has to involve conflict nor loud arguments but is more about challenging each other. It is about getting one's personal beliefs on the table for the rest of the team to learn about the values and priorities of those embarking on this team journey together.*

And so it was that on this visit to a lodge (more like a woodsy resort, as there was an excellent spa and a golf course), we did begin our storming stage with the

DOI: 10.4324/9781003196976-4

aid of the Strategy Deployment (SD) process. Strategy Deployment is another term for Hoshin Kanri, a well-established Plan-Do-Check-Act process that aligns the organization around the specific actions your team will do to achieve breakthrough levels of performance.

Every division in our company was required to have a strategy deployment matrix. It flowed from the Corporate Strategy, through the major product groups and business functions into the divisions responsible for profit and loss. It ultimately led to the stretch goals that ended up on an individual's annual goals and objectives as part of the personal performance plans. It was a well-established process in the company, albeit more effectively implemented in some parts of the organization than others.

I was a true believer in the process. (Let's face it, as leaders, there are many corporate initiatives we must implement with varying levels of enthusiasm.) I believed in this process to the core of my being. In my previous role, I had learned the process from our Corporate Sensei, Mark DeLuzio. It truly was a game-changer to enable a company to change its levels of performance on items of strategic importance, working ***on*** *the business, not just* ***in*** *the business.*

If done correctly, the company's top leadership examines the environment in which it operates and the levels of performance it wants/needs to achieve to be successful in its markets. As a collective team, it establishes its annual improvement priorities, which are customer-focused, are multi-year, are multi-functional, are process-oriented, and will result in new ways of doing business. As the goals and targets are cascaded through the company, there is alignment to the corporate goals and room to add any specific areas of focus a particular business needed to achieve its profitability goals.

The trick to this whole process is to start at the top and not have too many goals. It is sometimes misused as a laundry list of all the actions an organization must do. When everything is important, then nothing is important. This process strives to highlight critical areas but is not necessarily urgent to delivering value to the customer daily.

I had been the corporate owner of the process, which meant that on an annual basis, I facilitated the workshop that included the top 20 leaders of the company (minus the CEO, so there was no undue influence of the "big boss"), picking no more than 5–7 initiatives to cascade through the company. This was a journey, as we started with 10–12 initiatives and challenged ourselves to get better at prioritizing through the years. We reviewed progress on the annual improvement priorities (AIPs) from the previous year and decided if they had resulted in new ways of doing business and improved results. If they had, the AIPs became items removed from the current strategy deployment matrix to be sustained, and new priorities were added. AIPs could also be removed if they were no longer of strategic importance; however, this was rare. The leaders were held accountable for the progress of these items through quarterly reviews.

I fondly remember the workshops where I facilitated identifying the annual improvement priorities during the five years I was in the role. I had to get the 20 knowledgeable, A-type leaders of the company to agree on a small list of priorities. It was quite the cast of dominant characters. Fortunately, I learned a few skills over the years on how to keep this group, with the attention span of gnats (I say that respectfully, as they are all used to making big independent decisions multiple times daily) focused and on task.

As you can imagine, the room was 100% filled with BIG personalities. Ground rules for the meeting had to be established and agreed upon. It was important that I met with each of them ahead of the meeting so I had a feel for what bombshells may arise that could derail us. I even had to come up with secret keywords for a couple that would keep them in check, should an emotional outburst be imminent. We agreed to discrete code words ahead of time, and they knew I had to do it for their own good in the political scheme of things at the top of the company. I also scheduled the meeting for four hours on the meeting invitation, knowing I would be able to lead them through the process in three. As supreme overachievers, they always wanted to meet the goal in less than planned time, and every year they were appreciative of the hour I returned to them so they could get on with other important work that awaited them. My parting phrase was, "I have given you back an hour of your life. Use it wisely." We never left a meeting without our AIPs identified, and the CEO knew his top leadership team was aligned on the strategy. Boom.

Now you understand why I believed with every fiber of my being in this process. So, my team developed its annual improvement priorities for the fiscal year before any frivolity was to be had at our celebration weekend away.

This is not a how-to manual, but there are some key points I need to make that underscore the importance of this process and the business transformation we are recalling for you. First, our goals flowed from corporate goals/performance targets. Second, there are key business initiatives beyond lean implementation that must be considered, as resources are allocated and goals established. The lean initiatives are broken down into specific process development and implementation to support the transformation to a lean enterprise. Some of these initiatives overlapped with the teams formed by Rick, while others were independent of that effort. There needed to be one clear owner of each annual improvement priority, represented by the solid black dot. Many of these AIPs overlap, so many of the leadership team were on multiple teams, but only one "sheriff in town" to facilitate team success. Also, every person in the division who was either an individual contributor or a leader was assigned to a team. It was imperative to include everyone, so there was buy-in. As news of this spread through the division, there was much wailing and gnashing of teeth; nobody felt like they had 10% of their time available to incorporate this activity. After three years and numerous accomplishments that made their lives so much better, everyone wanted to contribute. Anyhow, we had left the annual celebration meeting at the lodge with great memories and our roadmap for the fiscal year.

Our Passion for Safety

Early on, I also established my firm conviction (maybe even fanatical conviction) to providing a safe environment for all our team members in which they work. My biggest fear was getting a call that someone would have a serious accident on my watch. This fueled my passion for cleaning and organizing everywhere to eliminate trips and other types of hazards that lurk in an environment where everything looks abnormal. We did so many things over the years to promote safety, but it started with a lot of communication. I ended every call or meeting with "thank you and be safe." I went on safety walks myself. We discussed near-misses as well as accidents at all the plant meetings. I put a safety goal on everyone's performance appraisals. When an accident did occur, it must be followed by a phone call to me once the order was restored, a containment action within 24 hours, and a review of the irreversible corrective actions implemented through structured problem-solving two weeks to the day after the accident. The entire staff had to participate in the review. Staff members on-site attended a pre-meeting in which we donned steel toes and safety glasses and went to the incident site. We reviewed what had happened with the injured employee (assuming he/she was back at work). These were mandatory meetings, no excuses. The only exception would have been a customer emergency. I would take attendance and have my Administrative Assistant chase down those who were late, which happened less often as the process became sustained and the team recognized the value.

In particular, my Marketing Manager expressed his irritation at having a safety goal on his performance plan and taking part in these reviews. I adored him and liked to create an inclusive environment, but this was nonnegotiable. As time went on, he begrudgingly participated, and we found that he often had the most creative/innovative solutions to supplement the team's work. He was a rock star at it, and as the recordable injuries in the plant began to decline, he became less grumpy about participating.

Early on in our safety journey, I found myself utterly frustrated with people getting hurt as a result of making decisions to take risks. Familiarity with an environment, I find, lends itself to thinking that nothing bad can happen to them. Sloppy practices, workarounds, using unsafe tools for the job one is performing, taking shortcuts, and ignoring personal protective equipment (PPE) requirements can lead to failure modes causing injury. As I discussed my frustration with my husband over dinner (our kids thought our discussions were not normal dinner conversation topics), he reminded me of a speaker he had once heard who had a heart-wrenching story about an industrial accident that ruined his life. We went online and found a video that could be purchased in which he relays his story in vivid detail. I bought a copy for every plant in my organization and required 100% of employees to watch the video. A funny story, funny as in ironic, not "ha-ha" funny, happened as a result of this video debut.

As it so happened, I was out of town at a Senior Leadership Meeting the day the video was shown back at the plant. The Plant Manager called me repeatedly several times. He never did that unless it was serious especially when he knew I was in the Senior Leadership Meeting. I politely and quietly excused myself from the room to call him back (awkward). He asked me to sit down, and when I had promised that a chair indeed supported me, he told me that one of our engineers had to be taken to the hospital to get stitches. The description of the injuries that were in the video caused him to feel faint. He got up to leave the room but did indeed pass out, cracking his head open on the frame of the door exiting the conference room. I tell you this because a career in manufacturing leadership is filled with things you cannot make up (cue the ibuprofen bottle). Even with an active imagination, being proactive with everything you can think of, and having the energy to prevent, stuff like this will happen. I couldn't believe it. I asked my Plant Manager what he wanted to do; did he want to stop showing the video? He was a courageous leader and believed in what we were trying to do. He insisted we carry on. He added that he would introduce the video and warn people that if they had an adverse reaction, they were to put their head down and stay in their chair, and someone would promptly and safely escort them from the room. I believe the testimonial in the video made an impact on the team. I also think it was good that this engineer realized his sensitivities to graphic medical situations, as we learned his wife was due to give birth within a couple of months. This unfortunate incident at work may have prevented an unfortunate incident in his personal life. We will never know.

We cycled through stages of being heavy-handed about safety incidents to being creative and upbeat about proactively promoting safety. Whenever an incident did occur, whether caused by poor judgment or unfortunate circumstances, the injured employee was sent to a local clinic and tested for illegal drugs in their system. If they refused or tested positive, there were severe implications regarding their continued employment.

However, fear is not a motivator that I find all that effective, plus I would never want to deter someone from reporting something unsafe. So we did our best to motivate people through alternate means of more light-hearted awareness. We launched one campaign involving life-size cardboard cutouts of me and three of my staff members dressed in proper safety gear. In these cardboard cutouts, we were holding clipboards to which we attached different safety messages every week. Our communications were tied in with these safety messages – sometimes tied to prizes if people could recite the theme of the week.

The cardboard cutouts were one of my favorite ideas, as we had a lot of fun with them. When they were first unveiled, people were amused with capturing them and putting them in strange places or near other team members, so it appeared as though the cutouts were watching them. Eventually, this game died down, and Cardboard Kathy was put in the lobby to greet visitors and remind them about being safe during their visits. I have many pictures of my employee's children posing with Cardboard Me when they came to visit their parents. I also have pictures of Cardboard Me in moose antlers at Christmas time. And there could be a picture of Real Me with Cardboard Me in matching Santa hats. The point is, we kept it fresh and amusing, drawing our team members into new ways of reminding them to be safe.

I tried to change my messages when I was walking through the plant to inspire people to be safe. Instead of getting angry when people were not wearing their protective gear, which was my first instinct, I talked with the supervisors about the superpowers that only I possessed to see people not wearing their safety glasses. When I asked people why they weren't wearing their safety glasses, and people would roll their eyes at me, I would simulate tripping over something and poking them in the eye. This would usually make them smile and cause them to comply (at least temporarily).

We also created annual safety calendars filled with our employees' children's drawings of their unique safety messages. The months were covered with colorful pictures about fireworks safety, crossing the road, wearing bike helmets, and my personal favorite, submitted by a five-year-old, not putting your hand in a machine. (I always hoped that youngster had some help from a parent.) We held a signing party, wrote personal messages to our customers and employees, and sent them out every Christmas. Not only did we send them home with our employees but we hung them up throughout our plants. The implied message was reminding everyone to work safely because not only did we care about them but so did people outside of the plant.

There are certain badges of honor every Operations Leader strives to achieve. You cling to them but don't want to say them out loud to prevent jinxing yourself. I cannot tell you how many safety celebrations I have heard of where a recordable injury record was broken the day after or, even worse, during a safety celebration picnic. For example, I had heard the story of a leader who decided to hand out steak knives to all employees as a thank-you gift (not kidding). And of course, someone injured themselves taking one of them out of the box.

My two unspoken significant accomplishments were that I had never shut down a car plant and that nobody had ever died on my watch. I know it sounds morbid, but I did have nightmares about either of those two scenarios. One night at dinner, Jeff and I were discussing industrial safety, as all typical families do, and I admitted to him that my worst fear was getting a call that someone in my operation was killed in one of my plants. He agreed. The kids, who were accustomed to such dialogues, rolled their eyes at what they had deemed one of my overly dramatic imaginary scenarios.

The next morning, I woke to at least five missed calls from my boss on my cell phone. This was most unusual. I called him back immediately and was informed that there had been a fatality at a nearby company plant. It was not one of my plants, but I was the closest member of management to the location. It was the call I had dreaded. And even though it was not technically my plant, it was still the worst work call I had ever taken. I immediately headed to the location. Most of the employees had been sent home, and the emergency responders had already handled the incident's most immediate impact. I remember the rest of that day vividly, as well as the next two days. I will not recount all the things as a leader you are trained in but not prepared for. I will share with you that I cleaned out the employee's locker with his immediate supervisor to return his personal effects to his family. It was by far the saddest act I had ever performed at work. It changed me as a leader forever. You can use fun ideas to promote safety and keep the message fresh, but safety is no joke.

Shannon

I came to realize that I had as high a level of passion for keeping our people safe as Kathy did, and I was equally as frustrated with our performance. After many injuries that year, I will never forget Kathy standing up in the conference room in front of the entire plant, pleading for them to fix the safety issues. We had invested in multiple different safety classes to open people's eyes and truly see unsafe conditions. We had been making good progress with 5S and starting to separate normal from abnormal conditions. The maintenance team was working like crazy to fix things, so why were we still having injuries? It was very frustrating, especially because Kathy sent all the right messages and reacted with all the proper urgency.

She was visibly upset during this talk, and I believe this was a turning point for the team. At that point, I think they saw the compassion she had for those getting injured and how much she cared about everyone in the division. That this whole thing we were trying to do with the lean and business transformation was as much about the people as it was about performance. All we'd been doing would benefit everyone involved, but we needed everyone's help. Everyone in the team needed to be talking about safety every day, reminding every team member about the importance of their actions. We had to help drive different thought processes and get our teams to have safety at the forefront of everything they did. They needed to own not only keeping themselves safe but look out for their team members as well. I can't remember exactly what happened after that talk, but I knew that the team would have followed her anywhere after seeing how much she cared about the people. Everyone in the plant got on board and started thinking about safety and our people differently.

Let the Training Begin

This was a turning point for me personally as well. I was starting to realize the type of leader I wanted to be. I cared about the results and how to achieve them, but I wanted to be a compassionate leader that made connections with the people I was working with. The relationships were quickly becoming what gave me energy, more than the business results, and I can thank Kathy for leading by example and helping me to see who I wanted to be.

I also realized how much I enjoyed teaching people and seeing them get excited about change and the idea that things could be easier, better, faster. In addition to learning and implementing strategy deployment and the safety training we'd been doing, we started teaching lean principles both in the plant and in the office. Investing in all of our people was important because we needed everyone to drive the transformation forward. The team neither had been taught how to do what we were asking them to do nor had been given the opportunity to do so. So Kathy asked all of her corporate friends that were available to help teach us as much as we could fit in, and it paid off in more ways than one.

We found that our teams were lacking basic problem-solving skills. I'm not talking about using the tools, although we needed that too, but about the thought process. We used the traditional A3 tool and the fundamental thought process to train our team members. It took time, a lot of practice, and coaching to apply both effectively. In my experience, it is essential to have someone on the team with the skill to ask questions and challenge the other team members to get as deep into the root cause as possible. The team needs to dig deeper into permanent corrective actions once containment is in place. This is critical to prevent a recurrence.

An important lesson I learned was not to put teams through a training class without a problem, process, or something related to apply during and after the course. These skills are not gained by listening to lectures read from PowerPoint slides but by applying them to something relevant in their world. Preparation for training involved identifying which problems to solve. There were many to choose from in both the plant and the office. They ranged from supply chain and employee turnover issues to material flow bottlenecks and equipment downtime. All were relevant to improving the current state. Most were chronic and able to be improved.

In addition to the technical skills being attained, we were also coming to realize that there were untapped skills in our team members that we didn't know existed. In one of our problem-solving sessions, we found that one of the accountants was skilled at writing macros and databases, something we needed in one of our teams. We had no idea she could do that. This is but one example of the power of involving everyone in these types of transformations. You never know where critical skills are going to present themselves. We also made the teams cross-functional. Having people outside of the departments where the issue exists leads to new eyes, new questions, and new ideas.

I was lucky enough to be on a problem-solving team with this structure. We had an issue with people getting injured walking up and down stairs in the plant. As we were trying to get to the bottom of this problem, looking at stats on the injuries such as department, shift, time of year, and amount of overtime, and we were finding nothing of substance. Then one of our team members, who happened to come from the accounting department again, said, "why don't we measure the stairs where the injuries occurred?" We all sat and looked at her. The thought had never crossed our minds. What we found was that the rise and run within a set of stairs were not the same. For example, one step could be eight inches high and the next would be five inches. How could that be? No wonder people were falling! We found that we had custom-built each set of stairs internally, with no specific standard, just making them fit the height needed. These makeshift steps not only varied within a set but between sets of equipment as well. As people went about their work on different sets of stairs, they could not develop muscle memory, so they were tripping and getting hurt. We went on from there to fix this issue in multiple ways, such as eliminating unnecessary sets of stairs and rebuilding sets with standard dimensions. How amazing to have a different set of eyes that does not go in the plant often comes up with a great idea that ultimately eliminated the safety risk!?!

I must add that both of these untapped talented people were women that were pigeonholed into their roles and never asked to participate in activities outside of their department. Maybe they weren't thrilled to be asked to be on these teams initially – they still had their day jobs to get done – but how many wonderful ideas and inspirations are hiding in our businesses that could be released if we only asked the questions or provided opportunities to contribute. Often, I have people thank me for including them on these types of teams because they felt that their voices and ideas were heard when they hadn't been before. How satisfying for all involved.

These were early challenges and early wins. While we pushed through this stage, challenges abounded on the home front as well. It was the first winter for Kathy in the lake house. It was an older home equipped with antiquated equipment for heating and water supply. One very frigid night, the heat went out. We were making numerous calls trying to find someone that could help us get it fixed and turned back on. After we tried everything that was recommended within the confines of the house, we reluctantly bundled up in winter gear and headed outside in our pajamas to unclog an air vent someone recommended we check. Imagine the two of us in the pitch-dark freezing cold, using a cell phone for light, poking at this hole on the side of the house with a broom. As there did not appear to be any airflow emerging from the vent, we figured it must be blocked. We were quickly caught up in a spiral of fear: "What if it was an animal?" "What if it attacks us?" "There's so much snow out here." "It's freezing." Then we started encouraging each other: "Ok, we have to do this." "Yes, we can do this!" And we finally got the courage to get closer and start clearing the snow. Luckily, no rodent emerged to attack us, and our efforts did result in the heat coming back on preventing us from having to relocate to the haunted hotel.

Kathy *It is from such adversity, whether at work with the wrong color tugger carts or at home nearly escaping death from frostbite or wildlife, that lasting memories are made.*

Shannon We were now months into this transformation, and I was traveling about 75% of the time to the plant where Kathy was headquartered. That plant had more challenging processes to work through and required more of my attention at that time. Remember that I was very newly married and not seeing Scott often, which was a significant change for us. I had to make a conscious effort not to get too sucked into the work or enjoying my one-to-one time with Kathy (and wine) to call home. If you've traveled, you may know that it's not always easy to have meaningful conversations other than "How was your day?" and "What are you going to do tonight?" Scott and I found that our frustration peaked when I was gone for four nights of the week. So I tried to stick to less than that whenever I could. It was lonely for Scott, and I lost sight of that sometimes.

I think this is a common struggle for many dual-career working couples, but I seemed to carry extra guilt being the one to leave all the time. Little would I know this would be the beginning of all the guilt I would carry throughout my career trying to balance family and work. Why is it that women carry all this extra guilt around with them? I wonder if when my male counterparts traveled, did they worry about how their wife was handling everything at home. If they were lonely? Or if they were able to just focus on their job at hand and not worry about what time it was or how much work they could fit into the day before they had to hit the road to get home? Trying to achieve this balance added so much extra pressure on me. I'm sure some of the pressure was self-inflicted, but we were told we could have it all, right? Having a strong work ethic had been instilled in me from my parents which made working hard a given, but keeping a happy marriage and throwing children into the mix was the challenging part. I realize that sounds backward, family should always come first, but I found this a difficult shift in priorities when all I had to worry about prior to marriage was focusing on work. I could write a whole book on work-life balance, but it's important to recognize the internal struggle that some women have trying to achieve this ideal vision of "having it all."

Personal challenges aside, we continued to train our teammates at every opportunity. The training paid off in many ways, and to me, this was probably the most valuable payback. Not only does the team get educated in topics and techniques outside of their traditional department but learning together also creates camaraderie. Spending uninterrupted time together, in a different environment, on a shared mission allows the team to learn more about each other as people, not just what they do for a day job.

Earlier in my career, I had attended many training classes that had icebreakers at the beginning of the session to promote teamwork. I have never liked them. The uncertainty of the surprise thing they are going to ask you to do or solve always made me cringe. I understand and appreciate the intent, and I am not suggesting that they shouldn't be done, just sharing my opinion on the matter. I do, however, thoroughly enjoy when the icebreaker is about getting to know that person. I've found that finding what motivates people and figuring out how to get them to work together is a strength of mine and something that gives me personal satisfaction. These icebreakers are a great way to do just that! You get to learn about your teammates in a different way, even if it is something as simple as what their favorite candy is or the first concert they attended.

The entire lean journey consisted of learning and development, as we were committed to getting everyone involved in our business transformation. Now it was time for us to go back to the closet and choose the next appropriate pair of shoes for the occasion ahead. Off with the trainers, on with the heels – time to strut our stuff in the office!

5

Stilettos – *From the Plant to the Office*

We were happy with how quickly the teams were picking up the lean concepts through the rigorous training plan we were executing to get everyone up to speed and contributing. It was imperative that the organization did not fall into the trap that these concepts only applied to the factory. So it was not long after the plant activities were well underway that we decided we needed to kick it up a notch and pull in the office teams. We didn't remove our steel toes altogether, but it allowed us to don some of those more fashionable heels that we hadn't had the chance to wear as often.

We would not only teach the concepts of 5S and how they apply in the office, but we would also start enterprise value stream mapping. Neither concept caused major excitement from the teams, but since it was not negotiable, they begrudgingly joined in, and we upped our energy and enthusiasm for them. These were significant changes we were asking them to try and be open-minded about, and none of it was easy. It was difficult and often frustrating work. But to achieve our goal of being a lean enterprise, it needed to be done, and we were determined to make it happen.

Office Value Stream Transformations

Kathy *Our division was mostly custom-designed products, so our Engineering team's effectiveness was critically important to our success. We decided to kick off a model*

DOI: 10.4324/9781003196976-5

value stream in that area. Let me tell you, people in the factories may not like it but are very used to being measured every which way to Sunday. People who primarily do "white collar" work, not so much. Again, the idea of "we are special, unique, and different" is alive and well in these types of areas. As luck would have it, our Director of Materials, Eric, was a very progressive individual, and he adopted the process wholeheartedly. This was essential to its success because while the application of the concepts to the value stream of "concept to launch" definitely apply, they are a lot more challenging to implement than those in the "raw material to finished good" flow. This would be the first of many value streams we would tackle, and each time once the teams got on board, they delivered excellent results.

Shannon

Starting with the "design to launch" process for our first office value stream transformation was critical to our business, and we learned a lot from it. We were fortunate that one of the Corporate Team members had gone through this same type of value stream transformation with another group with great success, so we had a reliable mentor to guide us. Kathy stated that these types of processes are much more complicated than the traditional "raw material to finished goods" flows, and she is 100% right. Completing value stream and process maps with the team were probably the most challenging mapping events I'd facilitated. The team was great, and we had the right people. The issue was that each person was doing the process a little differently. I think I said a hundred times, "ok, but what do you do typically?" so that we could get the process documented.

It was also interesting working through the difference in cycle times and lead times. Often, even with the mapping process on the shop floor, we want to make the tasks faster because it's tangible and makes us feel accomplished. When in actuality, that time is typically less than 1% of the total lead time to complete the process. However, there is still validity in doing this. For example, as a part of this current state discussion, one person would comment on how long it took to do a task, while another person's time was wildly different. We quickly learned that each of these slightly different ways to complete a task included slightly different ways of completing forms, documents, saving files, etc. This led the team to question why they were spending their time being creative inventing forms when we should be creative designing new products? So, as part of developing their future state, the Engineering Team set out to standardize templates and organizing techniques. This was time well spent. It led to each person completing these tasks the same way, intending to reduce the variation and the total lead time. An unintended, yet positive, outcome was by standardizing these processes, there were significant time savings during review meetings. It also fostered consistency when someone was absent.

For months the team went on following the same process we used on the shop floor as they worked toward their future state. They created value stream tracking centers, task lists, and teams. They held weekly value stream meetings and held each other accountable for success. This is where I created a fun pet project to help the team. While I continued to facilitate and ensure the team had everything they needed, I was not a material science engineer, so my ability to help with the tasks was limited. So, when the team struggled to figure out where they could have their "war room," the "super-secret room" light bulb went on. I had stumbled upon this room during one of our office 5S days. It was a room filled with years and years of file cabinets filled with paper, old parts samples, and stuff upon stuff upon stuff that very few people seemed to know existed, hence the name I aptly gave it. This was going to be the place! As I've learned about myself, I become a bit relentless once I set my mind to something. I was bound and determined to clean that room out and make it a useable space. I brought who I thought could be the natural owners of the documents and "stuff" to the room and pitched my idea. And no one balked at it. IT and Maintenance said they could get power and network in there, so I set up a few partial day events to start dispositioning all the items in the room. The room was very dirty, but the cleanup activity was so fun. Finally, the room was cleared out, and I got permission to get a computer and a large screen. I argued with the process owner that we should be having stand-up meetings and not sit-down meetings; therefore, spending money on tables and chairs was not required (I did lose this argument), and the room was ready to be unveiled. Of course, I created a PowerPoint with before and after pictures to share the transformation with everyone and what a little elbow grease and creativity could do.

In addition to the time saved by standardizing forms, the Engineering Team also created standard filing systems, so all of the projects were saved in the same format, and team members didn't spend time searching for files or being concerned that they didn't have the most current versions of the documentation. They also created daily meetings as part of their standard work, so interruptions were limited and productivity increased. A big cross-functional team project was initiated to consolidate tracking databases. Before there were three or four places where the same information had to be entered to get the data output needed, so they created one database where all pieces of data could be entered. It was a huge time-saver and productivity enhancer. Design guidelines were also established to ensure the engineers were starting with the same set of rules and not creating new ones at the start of every project. Finally, they acquired a tool that would take all of their work and automate many of the items they had put in place. Notice that the automation came last. The creation of the improved processes, tools, and techniques is so important to implement, understand, and use before automating. Doing this will make automation much easier because the team members know how the processes should function. So much time, effort, and commitment to respond to customers and launch products into the market faster went into this process. And as a result, new products were created and launched 30% faster than they were before! The team came to appreciate the standardization that allowed them to spend less time on documents and more time doing what would satisfy the customer and gain more business.

In another office value stream, which revolved around changing manufacturing work standards, the lead time was wholly driven by the backlog of change requests that had built up. The team could not work through it fast enough. This process was a crucial part of the quality system to ensure that all documentation was accurate to processing standards. The cross-functional team diligently worked through the same structured process of creating current and future state value stream maps, identifying the waste, and figuring out how to reduce it. One thing stuck out for me with this transformation. Once the team worked through the backlog, they effectively removed one person from the process and reduced lead time by 58%. The question remained: how do we prevent ourselves from getting backed up again? On the shop floor, we were asking that same question and putting visual controls in place to see normal from abnormal immediately. If it was working there, why couldn't it work here? We played with a few manual concepts at first. By now, you have probably picked up that I am a huge proponent of doing something manually first and working out the bugs before investing in technology. So we tried the manual tracking for some time, then progressed toward a giant TV screen in the office. It displayed where each piece of "inventory" was in the process and who owned it at that point. In this case, the "inventory" was the change request form that needed to be completed. Team members were notified via email when they had responsibility for a specific task. Expected completion times were established and added to each person's standard work. If an item was held up at one step or person for longer than that expected time, it changed color on the screen. I absolutely loved it and may have done a little dance when this went into production. Others may not have been quite as excited to have the entire office see that they were the ones holding up the process. However, after a while, it became second nature. It was not about shaming or punishing but allowing the other team members to step in and help when needed. It was all for the greater good, you could say.

Long after I left the process and the team continued to live it, I would receive emails informing me how great it was working. They were able to successfully maintain the levels they wanted. The team felt empowered and thrilled with the new system they had created, and this required task didn't weigh on them any longer. They had built success into the process. Not only did they feel great but I did too. It was amazing to get such great results and learn yet another part of the business that I wasn't familiar with. The best part for me was getting to work with people I typically didn't have the chance to. It was a privilege to get to know what their jobs were like and who they were as people. It was a great team to be a part of, and the fact that they wanted to keep me updated on their progress meant the world to me.

Office 5S

Kathy

At the same time we were kicking off office value stream transformations, it was also time to initiate 5S in the office areas. This went over like a lead balloon. However, never waning from my requirement that it must be done, I found a way to make it fun. Or, at least, I found it amusing. I started the tradition of making the 5S process an event. It was announced well ahead of time so people could manage their other commitments and this half-day would not interfere. Most of the office where I was located was a massive sea of cubicles, not with soft walls that went to the ceiling, only half walls where you could see how busy everyone appeared just by peaking around the corner. The expectation was that all the office employees would spend four hours "cleaning" up their area on Office 5S Day. I'm not just talking about wiping down surfaces, although that was included. This was meant to be a comprehensive review of everything in their space. Going through files and discarding unneeded papers and removing unnecessary items from their area. Does one really need multiple staplers in one cubicle? Then organizing said space, so the most needed items are easily accessible, and finally cleaning the area, so everything shines. There are two main reasons I made this a requirement. The first is setting a good impression for visitors or customers that we are organized and know what we are doing. The second is, if you know where everything is, it can be quickly accessed since all of the clutter is gone, and you can be much more productive.

Getting everything ready for the big Office 5S Day was equally important. We brought in dumpsters, yes, actual dumpsters, because experience had taught us that the small garbage cans were never large enough, and we didn't want to deter anyone from throwing things out because of space restrictions. We created a "red tag" area, a designated space to put items that were good and could possibly be used by someone else productively (even though there was no red tape or tags involved, it still worked great). We bought pizza for everyone. There was a bell in the office area that had previously been reserved for when a significant sale came in, and although it was not the traditional reason to ring the bell, I thought it appropriate to use it for this event as well. After all, installing another bell for the 5S event kickoffs would actually add to the clutter and therefore detract from 5S. I was always so excited to kick the day off. I would ring the bell with all kinds of vigor, smile gregariously from ear to ear. I would explain where the dumpster was, told where the red tag area was located, and assured everyone that I would be around to audit their process toward the event's end. I often closed with some pop culture phrase like "may the odds be ever in your favor." People worked hard to keep somber faces with little to no reaction, as they were not sure what to make of the unfolding events, never having experienced such an exciting work event. Usually, though, my parting line made them smile, at least the younger among them, reinforcing in my mind that I was still cool. (I had learned this trick in my early leadership days speaking to a group of interns. They warmed up to me as a leader/human being when I made a reference to the "loser sneeze" from Lizzy McGuire.)

The audits were my favorite part of the whole process. I went to each individual, asked them what they had worked on, and gave them positive feedback and ideas for the next steps. I asked them how they felt; what they learned. We laughed a lot. There was a lot of positive energy. I also learned of many well-kept secrets such as the super-secret room that contained mountains of banker's boxes of obsolete documents, the undercover pop cooler business being run by the Divisional Accountant, and the secret staircase that led to lofts of treasures. I found where all of our material experimental records were kept.

The best part of the day was when I audited and took the "after pictures," each person got a sticker for his/her badge. These were stickers like we used to get in Kindergarten for a day of good behavior, except there were more types of stickers available than the foil stars we all worked so hard to achieve. I always enjoyed picking out stickers for the events and tried to find ones that were small enough to fit on the security badges but also thematic for the time of year. I found shamrocks, smiley faces, and of course, I did not prohibit the multi-colored foil stars. I figured they evoked some sort of repressed positive feelings from everyone's yesteryears. People never refused the stickers. Even the team's most reserved and grumpy would open their wallets, get out their badges, and pick out the color/design they wished to sport. I loved it. 5S is essential for so many reasons. The event really brought the team together and established a tone of productivity, fun, and the future. It let the office people know that the lean tools were not just for the factory; they were indeed for all of us, and we were all in this together.

Shannon

Just when I thought it was tough teaching hundreds of people about the importance of 5S, we started in the office. Thank goodness for Kathy's unrelenting energy and excitement around this topic, or it would have been even worse than pulling teeth to get people to do it. If the stickers, ringing of the bell, and actual dumpsters weren't enough to pull people in, we hoped the free lunch would. All of this led to four hours of me walking around making sure people were actually working the process. It was difficult for them to step away from "real work" to "clean," which I, of course, explained that 5S is so much more than that! Insert grumbling and eye-rolling from a few. As we approached the four-hour mark, Kathy and I would ask each person to show what they had done during that time and what they had learned. I did my very best to keep the energy up and provide positive feedback and suggestions for next time (I know, I just couldn't help myself). I then presented them with a sticker of success, and they breathed a sigh of relief. Most of these encounters were positive, but not everyone was thrilled about this experience. As I was chatting with a team that was a bit secluded in an upstairs office space, one individual shared with me that this was the stupidest thing he'd ever done in 30 plus years. Needless to say, he did not want my super fun sticker.

As you can see, Kathy and I had slightly different experiences during this process! After our initial success and getting some positive feedback from the team, we (Kathy) decided to make this a quarterly event. It was an exhausting day for me, but I will admit I enjoyed seeing the people unite and get into the spirit each time we did it.

Once we got deeper into the rhythm of this process, we decided to take it to the next level. We created teams, and each one appointed an Office 5S Champion. That person would help audit the other groups, assign action items to their team members, and lead their teams to be the best 5S team in the office, which also led to pizza parties and other sorts of celebrating a win. You will quickly learn that Kathy and I really enjoy friendly competition!

So much good came from our office 5S days. It wasn't just because the office looked cleaner and more organized, but because the entire team was coming together in this transformation effort.

Establishing Traditions

Kathy

One of the things that always warmed my heart about being a mom was when my children would talk about memories we had made while they were growing up. Whether they were the traditions around holidays or the activities we would do like singing along at the top of our lungs to girl-power songs in our family room, I had fond memories like that of my childhood as well. So, I am a big fan of creating traditions and celebrations with those who I am surrounded by in life. I always view the teams I lead as an additional family, so I want to create those special moments with them as well.

Creating traditions or planning celebrations does not need to be elaborate or expensive to be meaningful! What is required about celebrations is that they do, indeed, occur. Life is short. And, in my opinion, too short. We can get so caught up in the grind of the days: the obligations, the quest of the next promotion, the merry-go round of completing one project only to move on to the next challenge without taking a break, without recognizing all that is good in those on the ride with us, and without taking a breath. Celebrations make space for all that nourishes our souls, our accomplishments, a pause from the ride, and a moment of gratitude. Celebrations bring affirmations, create memories, and allow us to see our teammates in a new light – one where the glow of positivity can prevail.

While official celebrations had always been part of my professional experience, the monthly team birthday cake, the suggestion award celebration, the work anniversary handshake, I came to appreciate the value of a good holiday party from one of my earlier bosses, Joe. Joe was the Plant Manager when I returned to work as a Manufacturing Superintendent seven months after my second daughter's birth. Every year he threw a great Christmas party at his house, and he invited the whole leadership team. Food was upstairs, and the bar was in the finished basement. His wife was the consummate holiday decorator, and the place looked like a Christmas museum for which tickets could have been sold. We had such memorable evenings. Evenings to laugh, get to know each other's partners, eat, drink, and feel the gesture of appreciation he was extending to us after a year of really hard work, perseverance, and grit. Fun was had by all, and none of the parties became topics of the annual ethics training, although, admittedly, these were days long before everyone carried a camera on their cell phones with them.

It became a tradition that we all looked forward to. If you aspired to leave Operations and go back to the promised land of Engineering or Purchasing (as we regarded them), you were still invited to the party, which was held the first Friday night of every December. You had been a brother in arms, and you were still part of the troops, a vital part of the tradition.

And so, having a team again in which a large portion of them was close to where I lived, I felt strongly that this was a tradition I should start. So, I invited everyone who worked in the offices and their significant others to a holiday open house at my home and started the tradition that would grow over time and become a part of the team cadence that we all looked forward to every year.

Admittedly, not everyone could logistically be a part of that tradition because of the division being spread out in four different locations in two different countries. So, I established another tradition where I sent a birthday card to each employee on the team. In it, I wrote a note of appreciation, celebrating the day of their birth and wishing them another wonderful trip around the sun. I was surprised by how much this small gesture meant to people. Once I started this tradition, I never stopped.

Those early days were crucial for establishing the type of leader the team would come to know me as. Living my values was always very important to me. I value trust and compassion and strive to be fair and objective in all circumstances. Although Shannon was staying at my house, it was important that she be treated the same as all the other staff members and not be perceived as a favorite. I came to appreciate some of the parental wisdom I'd gained over the years – you love them all differently, but none of them can be perceived as being the favored one. So, these were the early days in which this era was to be characterized by the early traditions we created. Some were directly associated with improving the business; some were directly associated with building a team. All were about bringing out the best contributions of all team members – letting them know they were essential to the business, to the mission, and to me.

We had gained momentum in the office, learning how to celebrate and create traditions as a team, but unfortunately, not all areas were having as much success moving forward. We would strive to keep the progress going, but soon we would have to wade through some storms to get all areas back on track.

6

Rain Boots – *Weathering the Storm*

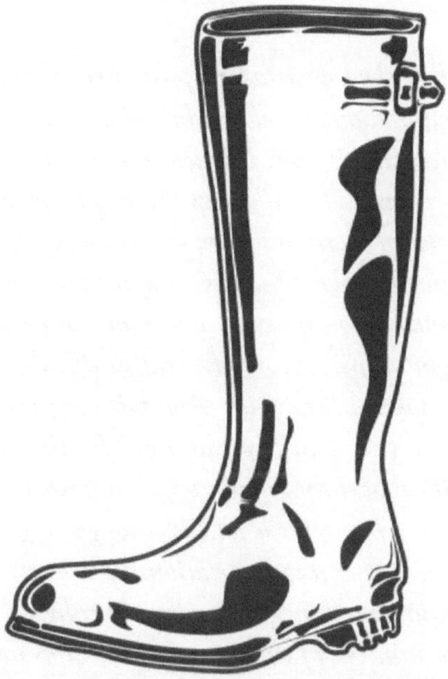

Momentum was building. In the first nine months, we had established priorities, filled the leadership team, and started the traditions of what would be our era. The lean transformation was squarely underway, with Rick Harris and Shannon leading the charge through a regular drumbeat of monthly daylong sessions and rigorous homework assignments. The thing about really changing a culture and leading a transformation is it requires resilience. No matter how articulate you are at painting the picture of a much better future state, the people you are describing it to have never lived in, nor seen, such a state. It is hard for them to imagine, and most are inherently sure that those leading the transformation do not understand the challenges of their unique business and all the reasons that it just won't work there. They are generally following along, reluctantly, because of the hierarchy of the organization chart. While they wish this future state, as described, really did exist, it is just hard for them to see how we will get from where we are to this so-called "better place."

Included in this future state is to see how we can utilize our people differently to become more productive. This would take hours upon hours of observation on the plant floor and using operator balance charts to truly understand what it was our people were doing. It would

DOI: 10.4324/9781003196976-6

allow us another opportunity to involve the people to make their jobs easier while servicing the customer at a higher level.

The next step we would need to unravel and redo would be how to schedule the plant. This would be the culmination of all of the work we'd been doing around material and information flow up to this point. It would lead to many frustrations and trial and error to get it right, but we would be firing on all cylinders once we could figure this out.

We would wade through storms of varying shapes, sizes, and degrees to keep moving down the path toward our future state.

Developing the Team

Kathy

It was my job as the leader to help push them through the chasm of this future state that they just couldn't imagine was achievable. I had to stay involved. I attended every hour of every Rick Harris visit. I reviewed homework on the floor with Shannon and the team between visits. I challenged the team members, and I celebrated the small victories. It is a lot of work to set the foundation, and you must put in a lot of effort before results come into play. There is a tipping point where that boulder you have been pushing up the hill reaches the crest, and momentum starts to accelerate as the boulder goes downhill, but at first, it is really, really difficult. And more than brute strength is required. It also takes a little faith. And faith requires trust. Although my philosophy has always been to give trust freely as a gift for the recipients to lose, I find that most people are not like that. I think most people require trust to be earned in the first place. In either scenario, when trust is lost, it is tough to get back, if not impossible. So, the early days of the leader and team relationship are critical. Any misstep in communication or deed would slow things down dramatically.

I had done a number of these transformations before, in both direct leadership, such as the Operations Superintendent or Plant Manager, to supporting them from the side as a member of a lean support team or the leader of a company's operating system. From these experiences, I found a trend regarding the hierarchy of adoption of the principles (if one is not already a lean zealot). Generally, the Plant Manager is skeptical, as he/she has gained their position through achievement in more traditional batch manufacturing and command/control methodologies. When a company is behind a lean transformation, they know that not showing some level of compliance, even perhaps feigned enthusiasm, would be career suicide. The people making the parts, or providing value, are generally all-in once they understand what is happening and why. Sure, you have the grumpy person who has worked there for 30 plus years and outlasted many a leader and many initiatives. Still, I find those people to be passive at worst, never really rebellious or undermining. The most challenging group to convince and convert is the first-line supervisor. Their power lies in managing the chaos. They have to take the fallout from the troops once the generals have gone back to their quarters. They must make something work that they may not understand fully. They look to their leaders (middle managers) to see their adoption of this effort and determine their loyalty to the cause based on their leaders' level of acceptance. It is not in the meetings, where generally, everyone is on their best behavior. It's in the team meetings that take place later; the floor walks when the higher-ups are not around, the 1:1 "what do you think about this lean stuff?" conversations, where the real truth comes out. If the Plant Manager is not all in, and many times they are not, particularly at the beginning, there will be divided loyalty among the plant staff at best, flat out rejection at worst, and passive aggression as a middle ground. It slows down the effort and creates a cold war in the facility. The Plant Manager must get on board.

With my personal trust model, as described, everyone has a seat on the bus. I am taking everyone on the ride to school. I want them educated, participating, and safely returned to their homes each evening. In the two, first and largest of the four plants we were converting to lean enterprises, there were many challenges with the upper levels of the plant management. They included a lack of faith, which led to a lack of execution. Now, let it be said that everyone gets multiple opportunities to get with the program. I know that the homework assigned each month was more than anyone could possibly execute in four weeks while making thousands of parts each day. I also knew that some of the items assigned may or may not make sense as other parts of the plan were executed. You learn as you go. I was ok with that. I was ok with confusion about the assignments and asking for clarification. However, after nine months of working on this, I was not ok with not trying to make the tools work or executing the manufacturing discipline basics in the plants regardless of the transformation underway. After one particular plant visit with Rick, following numerous individual conversations with members of the leadership team, I heard one of the first-line Supervisors say word-for-word a quote that was skeptical about the path we were on. Her words were the exact same words I had heard from one of her leaders. I knew we were not ever going to transform this business if the plant leadership was knowingly, or unknowingly, undermining me every step of the way. Some people do not choose to go on the journey and need to get off the bus.

Shannon

Oh, the puddles we had to wade through! At least I had the cutest rain boots to wear while I did so! In fact, there is a picture of me that I was unaware was being taken, in my colorful rain boots and dress traversing the sidewalk in front of the plant through a literal rainstorm. Inside the plant, storms were also brewing. I felt like I was fighting an uphill battle trying to get the team to come along when someone was in the background reminding the team that "they weren't stupid and what did "she" know anyway?" ("She," in this case, refers to me, not Kathy, although, in reality, it could have been either one of us.) This was an actual conversation I overheard in the office next to mine, unfortunately. I was already feeling isolated, and those comments solidified it. No matter what I did, said, or how often I was talking with the team and trying to help, I couldn't win as I, too, was being undermined every step of the way. As Kathy mentioned, everyone is given a seat on the bus if they want it. Not everyone has to believe, trust, or have faith in what we are doing initially, but they cannot block the way for those who want to progress. Once some people decided not to be on the bus with the rest of us, the storm clouds dissipated a bit.

Kathy

Things weren't all sunny skies outside of work either. I still had my daughter Claire at home, an eighth grader. I was commuting from 2 hours north of my permanent residence to make sure I spent at least 50% of the week with her at home. I loved being her mom and put as much energy into that role as I put into work. I put millions, ok, maybe just tens of thousands of miles on my car, driving back and forth to spend time with her and be an integral part of her life.

Her father and I were a modern sort of divorced couple. We were committed to co-parenting as seamlessly as possible for the girls' sake. We were not the "let's do holidays or vacations together" type of divorced family. But we were the school conference together, sit for recitals together sort of divorced family. And we both loved our girls fiercely and wanted to support them in living their best lives even though we were no longer together.

Claire did not always appreciate the loving guidance I enveloped her in, either from home or from my remote workplace. One day she got so mad at me because, during a geography lesson in which her teacher was projecting material from his laptop, an email popped up on the screen from me inquiring if she had remembered to turn in her project about Mexico. In all fairness, I guess that is not super cool when you are in middle school. But, whatever, making sure she was successful was part of the job description, so I persisted with my loving "support." I would spend some of my lunch hours assisting her with research for school projects so I could continue to be there for her even at a distance. She knew that I was her mom first, her friend second, always. I did extend my support by teaching her valuable tools like how to roll her eyes so that her head stayed stationary and she wouldn't be detected if her teacher was behind her. I put her in karate lessons to gain self-confidence, and a little self-defense skill is always a good thing for a young lady. She was thriving in school despite my private emails gone public, which validated that all of my time and support were paying off. I was determined to spend as many of my waking hours as humanly possible to make sure.

On nights that Shannon stayed at my lake house, there were many times she ate alone. I worked late hours when I was at the plant and not at home with Claire. Shannon would sit patiently to ask about my day, as I went through long conversations with Claire about how her day was, if she had turned in her homework, and what she worked on with her dad. Then I chatted with my husband about his day and what was going on with his work. I would then call Emily to see how things were going at college. And then, I would sit down on the couch and chat with Shannon. She said it was exhausting observing all my activities. That made two of us! I knew her life eventually would look like this, with similar obligations and challenges. I hoped I was being a good role model for what real life looks like for a dual career working mother. There were sunny days, and there were stormy days; but on those rainy ones, I put on those boots kept on plowing through the puddles, and eventually, the sun always came out again.

Shannon

Another type of storm we would wade through was happening within the transformation. The three lean teams were still working diligently on the homework, but we were learning that it wasn't enough. Yes, we needed to put these processes in and utilize the tools, but we also needed to trust our gut and try things. We had to take risks and learn from our mistakes. The team was trying to figure out every detail of what might happen instead of getting 80% of the way there and forging into implementation. This quest for perfection was slowing us down, and we had to start moving faster. While one plant was doing a great job going through the intellectual pieces such as operator and machine balance charts, understanding the math, etc., they were not doing the implementation work. The other plant had the exact opposite situation. They were getting visuals in place, material flow lanes set up, and things moving around the facility, but they did not utilize the math and let the system speak to them, and then making adjustments from what they observed. Neither approach was worse than the other, but once recognized, we could get a little more uncomfortable and start moving faster. Rick Harris would tell us, "Live on the edge of out of control, but always in control." The team could see the improvements that were taking shape, and they were ready to adjust and make things happen. Part of moving faster was continuing to meet with the operators. We did so at least once per week to let them know what changes were coming. We assured them that all we were asking them to do was try. If it didn't work, we would change it.

Standards and Work Balance

We were still creating standard work for hundreds of processes, and working toward a 20% productivity improvement, so we needed to think about operator utilization differently. We were running machines and processes part-time, which is very difficult to do. Most plants are not good at that, us included. So, in conjunction with creating standard work, we created operator balance charts to illustrate the workload of our team members. It's important to know the level of work an operator is capable of achieving, but it's more important to know what that work consists of. Operator balance charts are an excellent tool for that. Once these charts were created, we could see where their time was being utilized, finding that most of it was spent on non-value-added activities such as walking or doing paperwork.

We needed to improve productivity. We also needed to flow material through the plant. This included inspecting the parts the same day they were produced. That didn't mean the specific part but the same quantity. The work needed to be balanced between operators to flow through the facility. To enable that we needed to start removing the waste. We shared the operator balance charts and our findings with each of the operators as they were created and asked for feedback. In most cases, they were surprised by how much time they spent on non-value-added activities and not actually making or inspecting parts. Generally, that realization was not welcome information. That customer mindset was making its way into their thoughts, and they knew the customer just wanted their parts. This waste was preventing them from satisfying them. This was when it started to get fun. The operators would bring suggestions on how to set up their work areas in the most efficient arrangement. They had ideas on how to reduce steps in the required paperwork. And as we, especially me, relinquished some control over everything having to be perfect, we let them try things out. If the changes didn't work, no harm was done. We would just make additional changes.

In some cases, this trial-and-error methodology may have slowed down getting to the end result, but the goodwill generated from empowering and engaging the team far outweighed any time that may have been lost. Now the operators had some ownership in the process changes, and you could feel the energy starting to shift. This sounds simple, maybe even obvious. However, it took many hours of observing, writing, and rewriting standard work, then using that data to build the operator balance charts to a format that we liked, and THEN convincing the team it was reality. Not at all easy, very time-consuming, but absolutely a necessary part of the journey.

There were other key observations that we learned from implementing this tool and process. The first was that we did not have standardized break times. Operators within a department would go to breaks at different times. We asked the Supervisors how they kept track of everyone's schedule. They admitted it was really difficult. This seemed like a pretty simple way to increase productivity, which it was, but it was time-consuming and required resources to get it done. We started by implementing break bells to signify the start and end of the breaks. It was mind-boggling how many of these bell sounds there were. We had to do some upgrades to the sound system, try different tones and volumes, and stagger the break times to ensure the ever-pressing need for microwave time in the break areas was sufficient. (Maybe not as simple as we thought!) However, it all paid off in full once implemented. It helped with the Supervisors' sanity as well. Now the entire department would come and go. They could hold their teams accountable, and everyone knew who should be where, when, and got that productivity gain we had been targeting.

Another observation that took us painfully long to get right was the shift change. The type of machines we had required an operator to be there once the cycle was over, or it created all kinds of subsequent quality issues. We instituted a 15-minute shift overlap that should have covered it but often resulted in the first-shift person walking away and standing around for 13 of the 15 minutes while the second-shift person struggled to keep up with startup procedures and get good parts off the machine at the same time. This was a very frustrating topic for Kathy and me, as we continually reviewed data on why we were missing productivity targets when the time was right there to get if we could only get this right. (There may have been an unpleasant "discussion" on this topic over the microphone one day, but let's just say Kathy's frustration hit its peak.) After a lot of trial and error (lots of minute-by-minute flip chart plans were in play here. As Kathy mentioned every minute lost is an opportunity to disappoint a customer), we finally created and documented a smooth transition. The operator balance charts were great at capturing this waste and the impact on the improvements we made.

We also learned that demand could change rapidly for the markets we served, so updating the charts needed to be done monthly. As we continuously improved our processes, we improved our data collection. We ended up linking the demand to the Plan For Every Part (PFEP), so everything was connected. Once a month, the PFEP was updated, which updated the demand in the operator and machine balance charts, and the EPEI calculation, which determined how many parts we would run each time we ran them. Finally, all of this would lead to updating how much inventory was kept in the markets. The math was connecting all of the processes in the plant! (Who knew this would be as exciting as it was?) We would then meet monthly as a team to determine where shifts in people or equipment needed to be made. After a few months of working on this process, it became second nature. We built the process into our management standard work, and we started to understand what the math was telling us about our operation and how to utilize it to improve performance.

Building Finished Goods Markets

While the Manufacturing Team continued working through understanding labor and capacity, the PFEP Team worked on building finished goods markets and how to schedule the plant. Both were critical to the success of the system. Creating finished goods markets absorbed some of the variability in plant performance and customer demand while we kept progressing through better ways to produce flow. It created stability. While inventory is considered a form of waste, it is also sometimes necessary waste to bolster stability. It is important to optimize the amount of inventory. Too much will bog down the system and add unnecessary costs to the business. Not enough will not allow processes to ramp up and flow or meet delivery requirements. Once the math was completed for each part number in the PFEP, it was determined that we had too much inventory of some parts and for others not enough. This information would be critical in physically sizing the market appropriately. More to come on that.

The math told us specifically how many pieces were needed in the market of each part number. However, we still needed to figure out what our capacity would allow us to produce on a daily/weekly basis. We needed to add parts to stock as fast as possible, so we created a Gantt chart to track progress. What is complicated about this is needing to run current customer demand and what the finished goods market requires at the same time. We tracked how many parts needed to be produced weekly to achieve both goals. Of course, we had the best intentions to stick to this plan, but it is manufacturing and things tend to go awry from time to time. (Remember the giant bottle of ibuprofen?)

To achieve the goal, we utilized our visual control principles and built in a weekly review at our value stream tracking center meetings. If we got off track, we would develop countermeasures to make more parts. Overtime was an option, but we also looked at utilizing other machines and running some parts on multiple machines simultaneously. Another option was to cross-train more people in that department as we were freeing them up from all of our waste removal efforts in other areas of the plant. We were pushed to be creative, to consider all options before turning on overtime. It was uncomfortable and seemed impossible, but you would be surprised what a great team can come up with if given boundaries and pushed a little!

To add another level of complexity to the process, we also had to figure out where and how we would store this additional inventory. This required a complete overhaul of our shipping departments in each of the plants. We were able to physically resize the department in one of the plants ourselves with a lot of sweat during a hot week in the summer. It didn't create too much interruption. In another plant, it required a more significant teardown and rebuild. It was a project that I had fun with, although I do recall an intern not being overly thrilled with me as I gave him my elaborate list of requirements. I had him come up with multiple layouts that required racks to be 7-ft tall or less for small boxes, sized to box height to eliminate air storage, and weight restrictions to avoid heavy lifting outside of the correct ergonomic zone. Then add 10–30% extra space to accommodate demand shifts. Finally, we had to make plans to eliminate the loft area where we stored a ton of parts that had to be accessed by one single point, which required a forklift. The loft was home to one person that was performing incoming parts inspection. There were so many safety opportunities to address with this process. (Kathy made the lady who worked in the loft wear one of those "I've fallen and I can't get up" necklaces. Necessary, but still comical.)

As I added more requirements, the intern's eye-rolling and "this is impossible" comments increased, especially when I commented on what a fun project this was. (Insert silent giggle here.) He was a smart young man, and I knew he could do it! Another requirement was to place the most frequently used parts in specific warehouse locations, so the shipping person knew where to go most often and reduce the walking needed. This meant that infrequently used parts would have a separate, more general location. We had a couple of different options we used for the low-frequency parts, but we found the best was to create a shelf or shelves dedicated to a range of part numbers. While this wasn't a perfect solution, it narrowed down the needle in a haystack feel, and you didn't have to worry about rack space not being utilized because you didn't need to run that part this month. This project took over a month to complete. We completely emptied the warehouse, moving parts all over the plant. We created temporary storage locations and documented where every part went. We then hired an external company to come in and tear down all the racking and rebuild it to a very successful layout our intern had designed. (By the way, he did meet about 90% of the requirements, which was considerably more than I thought could actually be accomplished!) Then everything got moved to its new location (more sweat), and success was celebrated with a pizza lunch and a plant-wide presentation.

Kathy *I think she should have handed out stickers too!*

Shannon I say success not just because we had a fantastic, safer, more efficient layout but because there were zero safety incidents during this process. Not one part was lost, and we had zero delivery misses! This was a huge win, and once again, I was incredibly proud of this team. Now we just had to fill the market up!

Scheduling the Plant

During this time, the team was also trying to figure out the most difficult part, in my opinion, of the process yet – how to schedule the plant. At this point, there were multiple points of schedule. In fact, the parts got rescheduled every time they moved. We had to learn what the pacemaker was to know where our single point of scheduling was. It happened to be different in each plant, even though the processes were similar. The pacemaker is the point at which a part becomes a specific part number and can't be anything else, or the point at which parts can flow freely from there the rest of the way through the value stream. The value stream map is a huge help in identifying which process is the pacemaker. Once determined, we had to understand the best changeover sequence, so when Production Control put the schedule out for the day(s) or a week, they would do so optimizing changeovers. To do this, we had to work closely with the operators since they were already trying to optimize the sequence in which the parts ran. Once we had the optimal sequence documented, with their input, we formalized the "changeover wheel" and gave it to Production Control. It wasn't perfect at first, but we started scheduling with it and tweaked it as we went. The operators were very vocal when something wasn't right here because it made their job much more difficult.

As we progressed and improved the process, we found it would be much easier for Production Control if they could quickly identify which part went into which changeover category. Changeover categories were determined by part families that share tooling and equipment required to perform the setup. Our goal was to minimize the number of difficult changeovers. We created planner codes by changeover category and loaded them into our Enterprise Resource Planning (ERP) system. That way, when the work orders for that week were printed, they could quickly be sorted into the best changeover sequence. It was awesome if I do say so myself! Now the Production Control Planner knew what were difficult changeovers and could minimize the number of times they were required. Sometimes they were required to satisfy the customer. This is ok but cannot become the norm. The Planners need to understand the impact that decision makes on how much time and capacity is lost and work with manufacturing on how to recover it if needed.

There is a significant amount of learning that takes place while figuring out how to schedule correctly. I spent a lot of time walking through the changes with the team, listening to them vent their frustrations, and insisted I was only a phone call away (which I actually loved when they called because that meant they were trying!) We took steps forward and steps back during this process because of how much detail is required to understand every process's connectivity. The teams did get frustrated during these large changes, but the sign of a good team is to try, push through the difficulties, and try again. Start at the pacemaker and try process by process to walk through how it could work. Did I mention that everyone needs to TRY?

An important note on the single point of schedule is that when you have work-in-process (WIP) markets in place, they do not count as a scheduling point. One of our plants could not build WIP markets due to their product mix of low volume, high mix, and shelf-life requirements. But our other plant was higher volume, lower mix, and they were able to cycle through more standard parts faster, which lent itself well to implementing WIP markets. This was an easier model because you had a point of buffer between processes versus having to flow from the pacemaker all the way through. So, in addition to building finished goods, we also needed to implement these WIP markets. The process of building a WIP market is similar to creating finished goods markets, but it added a second loop of pull to work through and manage. They also required us to know the best changeover sequence and set up the pull board in that sequence. Instead of Production Control scheduling it, the customer's pull out of finished goods sent the trigger back to the point of schedule. This, in turn, took parts from the purchased components and WIP markets in order to make more parts and trigger the markets to refill.

Once we put this system in, the time to create the schedule each day went from 90 minutes to 15. The system told us what we needed to run; we just had to trust it. That's not to say we implemented, and it went off without a hitch; there were still many learnings and changes we had to make. But we started to let the boards talk to us and tell us when there was a problem. We would study the board and the pull cards on it and ask, "what is this board telling us?" Sometimes when nothing was triggered to run, we would say, "Oh, we are in great shape. The market is full, and we can utilize the people elsewhere," but it would also beg the question, "Why is the market full? Is the customer not pulling for a reason?" It's possible nothing was wrong with the pull from the customer, but it still forced us to think differently and ask the question. Other times everything on the board was triggered, which told us we had a problem. Is there not enough inventory in the markets? Did the demand change that we missed, and now the customer is pulling faster than we thought? Was the machine experiencing downtime or high levels of scrap? And also, what were we going to do to make more parts? It is a powerful process to be able to walk the floor and have the plant talk to you, taking the guesswork out of it. You don't need to have WIP markets to do this, but in this case, it guided us to expand this type of thinking. In the other plant where we were running everything by a first-in-first-out (FIFO) process, different visual controls were needed. Shortly, I will share our creative use of solo cups to help with this, and no, it does not involve your favorite beverage!

There are many good books on how to implement markets, so instead of getting into all the detail, I'll tell you about the super fun pull card making parties we invented! Maybe "party" is too strong of a word, but we needed to make this task fun somehow, and we had to recruit people to help! The books don't tell you how much time it takes to keep these pull systems going. Setting them up is one thing, but it's the monthly upkeep that we underestimated. They also leave out the inevitable paper cuts, sore fingers, and broken nails that you will endure (all worth it). As demand shifts, so should the number of cards in the loop, which means adding and removing cards each month (or whatever frequency is best for the business). One of our Production Control managers, Rick (we will call him the "other Rick"), took this process very seriously and developed a method to streamline it over time. He had a cart set up with all the tools needed and even created a golden sample, so those helping did it the same way each time. This was another improvement we made as inevitably, someone would get a bunch of cards made and realize they were upside down. (The tugger driver who was moving these cards was expecting the cards to look the same every time, which made the standardization of the process so important.)

Through trial and error, we discovered that printing and laminating the cards was not the way to go. It took forever and caused a lot of garbage. Instead, we went with printed cards that we folded in half and put them into plastic sleeves that could be reused. We also created a spreadsheet with a tab for each part number. Tedious to set up, but worth the initial effort to make the monthly updates, or even on-the-fly updates that much easier. We would then print whatever quantity was needed, cut them, fold them, and put them into the sleeves. When we took cards out of the system, we would just pull out the paper, recycle it and save the sleeves for later.

We found that each of us had special skills when it came to making pull cards. "Other Rick" excelled at cutting on the paper cutter; I was good at folding and stuffing the sleeves. I always say everyone has to be good at something; my special skill was stuffing pull card sleeves! When I took the cutting job, I would get lectured as "Other Rick" peered over my shoulder on how I was doing it wrong (insert eye-rolling).

The boards also needed to be updated with trigger points, and the number of spaces on the board moved as demand changed. The trigger point was tied to the run quantity for each part number and is the same as the EPEI we discussed earlier. This is where the cart came in equipped with a stapler remover, stapler, wet-erase marker, and the spreadsheet created to make the changes. It was quite the process and seems a little silly to write about, but the system would have failed without the diligence to ensure it was updated. It was also a time that we bonded and enjoyed each other's company. I remember someone asking me why I spent my time doing this when I probably had better things to do, but did I really? It allowed me to step back and see the system and determine what was working and what wasn't. It gave me time to think, which was rare those days. It also allowed me to spend time with the team, poke fun at each other, and laugh a little. So no, I didn't have better things to do. It was a requirement of the system, and it was a task I enjoyed!

If you are thinking at this point, "Wow, all of that is a lot of work," you are right. The teams were able to keep working this hard on the business instead of in the business because of the roadblocks Kathy kept helping us remove. Some roadblocks were a required part of the business, but others were distracting. Having a leader that understood that was a huge factor in our success. We were about to enter another milestone in our process, an annual distraction that took some of my focus away from our transformation but simultaneously took the team's confidence and trust in us to the next level.

7

Tap Shoes – *Dancing Through the Noise*

It had been an incredibly busy first year up to this point. And yes, we have spent this entire book talking about the first year. But stick with us because, with any lean transformation, it is all about the foundation. There was so much data to collect up to this point, and remember, we started with a model value stream in each of the two facilities we were focusing on. Once we learned, applied the basics, and began to get into the real substance of the tools, we started applying them across the business as quickly as possible.

While our extended team was driving the improvement through the business, the leadership team was putting on their tap shoes to dance through the annual planning process. This year the process would afford us the opportunity to share what we had been accomplishing with those higher up in the corporate hierarchy. They would get to see the work firsthand and decide for themselves if the strategy we had established as a team was really going to yield the results we claimed it would.

While we prepared for our live recital, transformation activities were still underway. New tools and processes were being implemented as part of the new normal. The team was getting used to an ever-changing environment. The challenge was to ensure sustainment for everything new that had been put in place. Layered process audits were the answer to this challenge. We quickly learned that if you don't audit a process, not only will it start to morph into something you didn't intend it to but you also may not capitalize on further levels of improvement. Both are incredibly important.

DOI: 10.4324/9781003196976-7

Requirements from Headquarters

Kathy *As a business leader, many stakeholders must be managed. There is Corporate: "We are here to help." There are initiative owners, such as the "wellness" owner: "Please remove your metal teeth fillings immediately." There are customers: "We need you to reduce your prices by 15%, or you'll lose our business." There are suppliers: "Hey, just to let you know, the factory that supplies your material just burned down." There are all the employees: "Kathy, can you get the ice machine fixed in the break room?" There are your mentors: "Kathy, you do realize these guys get diversity bonuses, right?" These, in general, are the external forces in your worklife that have nothing to do with the business transformation you are so passionate about. The one you are driving with your whole heart and soul so that your children's children will be able to support a family by working there if they should so choose. It is also the work that will prove that you deserve a seat at the table, which the senior leaders occupy. Shannon was the person leading this transformation for me – and I had to manage all the stakeholders to free her from these distractions. So, I put on my dancing shoes and entertained them so that she could stay focused on the ultimate mission. (Just so you know, I never did absolve her of her mail-retrieving duties at my house. She had to manage her time and earn her keep by extracting those spider egg homes disguised as stamped envelopes.)*

Shannon It really was not that bad – eye-rolling!

Kathy *I am a person who has served in different types of roles in my career. Before this role, I had been that person from HQ who showed up at the divisional doors to teach, assess, and provide feedback, even if it was not wanted. I was one of the people who had to come up with a compelling response as to why the locations that I visited should be doing lean transformations, even though 100% of them stated that they were unique and different, and many felt that these tools did not apply to them. The point is, I am not opposed to help from "Corporate." In many cases, there are some really smart people there who are experts in their field and can truly help you improve your business.*

There are times, however, when corporate requirements can be a distraction. One such annual process was so all-encompassing that even customers knew what time of year it took place. They planned their needs for attention outside of this time frame because they knew every internal organization was preoccupied with the production of slides. This process consisted of a comprehensive view of the business three-fourths of the way through the fiscal year. As a staff, you reported progress toward current annual goals, accomplishments, and challenges. You then presented your goals/initiatives for the following fiscal year. Upper management and your entire peer group attended each other's presentations. Our families knew when this time of year was, as many times getting physically to the presentations meant forgoing the celebration of your own Mother's Day, in my case. If you were "lucky" enough to be the host location, as I indeed drew the short straw for my first one, a year after I began to lead this business, you also hosted a tour of your plant. Your thanks for hosting this large multiday event was that "gift" of feedback from not only your boss but all your peers as well, including the previous leader of the business you were now running. Presenting improvements in such a situation is a bit tricky, as you do not want to insult the former leader with things like, "I can't believe how awful the 5S was in this plant a year ago."

While I was busy negotiating the performance goals for the following fiscal year in preparation for our team's presentation, Shannon was busy preparing her slides on the lean initiative. She was also preparing the plant for the big tour, a debut, of sorts, for our facility. This included preparing all of the presenters. We were determined that the people who did the work, made the improvements, generated the value daily, would present their work and accomplishments. Usually, the Plant Manager or members of his/her staff did the presenting. We wanted the people that had been empowered by the process to be the stars of the show. This meant that Shannon was helping numerous people along a choreographed tour route practice their talks. Most of the people had never presented to "dignitaries" before and were quite nervous. I did several dry runs with all of them myself. I wanted them to know that I had confidence in them and how very proud I was of their work during our first year together. It was so great seeing the "smile" factor and straighter postures emerge from my team members, as they had been given the opportunity to use their hearts and minds in addition to their hands.

It was also an important moment for my staff. I knew that this was a bit of an interview process for each of them. In some cases, this would be the only chance they would have to present their accomplishments to the group of people who had the final say in succession planning and their compensation. It was important that they shine. I wanted our presentation to be professional to represent the quality of work we were indeed engaged in. I hired a professional photographer to come in and take portraits of everyone so they would appear professional in the organization charts I would show. I specified an official required font so that our presentation would appear harmonious. (My team balked at that – but nothing is more annoying than one person presenting in Calibri and the next in Times New Roman – you lose continuity and attention as the brain adapts to a different typeset.) Instead of the standard 50 plus page slide deck that was produced, I felt there needed to be an additional entertainment factor so that we would stand out in our visitors' memories as being different and maybe even enjoyable for the first time our team had to present. I wanted it to be as memorable as my oldest daughter's first dance recital, "Barn Yard Bop," in which she tap-danced her heart out as a sequined tomato!

Sometimes my team was uncomfortable with my ideas, so I had to incorporate them stealthily. My Marketing Manager always advised me not to "poke the dog" when I went a bit untraditional on everyone. Whatever, this was MY team's debut. In between the excel spreadsheets and standard templates, it had to be unique.

The first thing I did was create a music video with pictures of our team's first year together: the celebrations, the hard work, the improvements, and office 5S days (my personal favorite). I am confident this was the first time a music video had been played during a budget review. This was followed up with a bit of a stand-up comedy routine about the double meanings of the new terminology I was learning about the industry – well, at least I found it amusing. With the crowd warmed up and the progress we had made, the presentation went off without a hitch. The tour was fantastic as well. I beamed like a proud Mama watching her child's first school play. It was magical. Even the "gift" of feedback was effusively positive. I was so happy for my entire team, especially Shannon. After the hard time I received about her taking the role, all the doubts were finally dispelled.

Shannon

In my previous role, I had experienced this comprehensive budget and planning process when the entire division staff would disappear for extended periods of time. Decisions weren't made in a timely manner, and we would attempt to do what we were already doing with many disruptions for data requests, slides to present, etc. Tap dancing through all this noise would become a much-needed skill during this process. I had not presented at one of these events before joining Kathy's team. What a new experience that was! I was more aligned with the Marketing Manager as "let's just get through this and do what they ask," but appreciated Kathy wanting to show who we really were and not just numbers on slides. We were early in our transformation process and had A LOT of groundwork to cover before the metrics would move in our direction, so it was important to show all the work that was going into this. Preparing the slides was the easier part for me, especially after learning about the font type requirements.

I would spend most of my time figuring out the tour route and prepping the team. As Kathy said, this was sort of a debut, and not only did I want to prove myself after the debacle and doubts in the hiring process but I had spent so much of my time training the team that I wanted to show that it wasn't just me doing the work. They are the ones who deserved the real credit. They were making the changes AND doing their day jobs very well. They were there during the previous leadership, and they had something to prove, too, that things could be different and their voices mattered. I spent hours setting the agenda, determining the presenters, creating the visual boards, and rehearsing with them. I had many reviews with Kathy because she was right, we had to tread lightly with how we presented. Her input was invaluable here. As in any learning process, she would give suggestions, and I would go back and try again. It could be frustrating at times, but I wanted to get it right for everyone. Before Kathy did a dry run with us, I would do at least two with the team. There was no way I was going to let them fall down or be too nervous to showcase their excellent work.

The long days I put in paid off in full. The presentation portion went very well, as Kathy mentioned. Her comedic routine about learning the new terminology in this part of the industry was a big hit, and our team's personal brand was born. When I got up to present, I thanked the Quality Manager who had been filling in for my role before I was hired. I recognized that he did a great job and was probably thankful to hand over the reins and focus on just one job. This was followed by a "You go girl!" shout-out from said Quality Manager. Our supportive and untraditional team's personality was publicly solidified. I was confident and believed in what I was presenting, so it was relatively easy. I felt good about how my presentation was received, but I felt great about how the plant tour went that evening. We had only arranged for 1 tour group because we expected 15 people (or less) to participate since it was at 6:00 pm. But I think so many people wanted to see for themselves if this "lean stuff" worked as advertised, that we had double the number we had anticipated.

I led the tour using our now famous microphone (and yes, backup batteries were safely tucked away in pockets), but I did very little of the presenting. The team did an outstanding job explaining the tools with confidence and sharing their experience going through the process. We had value stream managers, process engineers, team leaders, and operators presenting. All of them shared their personal views on what we were doing, and wow, it was powerful. I believe everyone on the tour that day shifted their thinking a bit after hearing what the people had to say. It was one thing to hear from Kathy, me, and the leadership team that we had buy-in, and the whole thing was great. It's another thing to hear it from the people on the floor and see it in action. Kathy was smiling like a proud parent, and so was I. I could not have been more proud of the team that day. After the tour, we got to hear the feedback on how upper management thought it went. We heard mostly positive comments about getting the right talent in place. It was obvious we were working on the process and strategy. The budget presentation was just a by-product of the positive changes we were making. The strategic alignment was impressive. Stay the course.

There were two pages of feedback that I had written down. This surprised me as it was almost 7:00 pm and we had been at this literally for 12 hours. But I suppose we weren't the only ones trying to prove our value during this annual process. The feedback actually felt like a true gift when received, and we left that day energized that what we were setting out to do was working and others were recognizing it. We knew we were doing the right things, and Kathy had worked hard to get the team aligned, so the validation was a big deal for everyone. It also gave our team a level of credibility that the metrics would move in the direction we wanted; we just needed a little more time.

Our team felt as great about the tour as we did. Kathy and I were copied on an email exchange from a couple of our frontline leaders who validated everything we felt. There was an appreciation for embracing the process and how hard everyone was working. There was pride in the work being done. The team felt valued in being a part of the transformation and were thrilled to see the people's mindsets changing toward the positive.

Kathy

This is what the transformation was all about: people making a difference and being part of something meaningful.

Shannon

The very next day I left for Italy. It was a year to the week since Scott and I were married, and with me traveling and working tirelessly on all of the above, we hadn't spent much time together. So, we decided to do a honeymoon redo since our original honeymoon was a bit of a disaster. The short version of this story is the trip consisted of a lot of rain in a place where it supposedly never rains, and locals told us, "This weather is so crazy! It NEVER rains like this." An excursion to the top of a volcano in the middle of the night to watch a sunrise that didn't happen because it was 30 degrees and, you guessed it, raining. "This only happens 10% of the time. You could try again tomorrow!" We had just biked down a volcano in the pouring rain, mud head to toe, and you want me to do that again? Um, no thanks. This was followed by me getting food poisoning, oh, and more rain. I recognize these are some first-world problems, but we worked really hard, saved up, and decided to try this romantic vacation to celebrate us again. So off we went on a dream vacation to Italy where I tried and tried not to check my email, but I wanted to be there for the team should they have any questions. Looking back, it was probably silly that any question could not have waited a week, but I did not want the momentum we gained from our visit to stop. In case you were wondering, we did have a fabulous trip that totally redeemed the first debacle of a honeymoon!

Back to Business

Kathy

With this planning season squarely in the rearview mirror, it was time to get back to business. And, as I explained before, not all business pertains to making parts. One of my favorite initiatives that all of the divisions were held accountable for was implementing a local wellness initiative. Our top leadership had a genuine interest in alternative medicine. Every team was measured to the extent that people took advantage of supplements, massages, pre-screenings, and gym memberships.

At a weekly call, I was required to attend to go over my production numbers; I was asked by my boss's boss what I was doing about all the obesity issues at my location. His exact words were "What are you doing about all of the fat people over there?" Unclear of an appropriate response, I chose not to respond, and just waited for the next unpleasant line of questioning to begin. This incident did cause me to change the lunch menus for his future visits. It was a small town and difficult to find caterers open during some of the seasons, much less ones that did not make their entire business plan around comfort food. But, with a few trips to the grocery store for apples and grapes replacing donuts and bagels, we were able to survive those future visits and keep him from doing a diatribe in front of the entire team about our height to weight ratios. I broke out the weighted hula hoop I had won at the senior leadership wellness fair and encouraged my team to use it during breaks and lunch. You had to use it with steel-toed shoes because when your hips could no longer keep it afloat, it really hurt when it landed on your foot. We bought pedals that could be used under people's desks to simulate bike riding while they were checking their email. After the first person bruised their knee on the bottom of their desk, those made their way to the red tag area in a subsequent office 5S event. We bought balance balls for people to sit on at their desks to replace their chairs and work on their cores and their product designs simultaneously. We eventually had to ban the balls from meetings because inevitably, we would have a bouncer or two that was distracting others from the topic at hand. My boss was progressive enough to let me get a treadmill desk, and I loved it. I was able to get my steps in during long conference calls and email checking.

We formed a Wellness Team to generate additional ideas that my Human Resources Manager led. One day he was summoned to Corporate for a meeting, and it happened to coincide with the free vitamin B shots they were distributing at the clinic there. I told him he should definitely take one of those free energy shots while he was there, but he should leave his cigarettes in the car.

This was one of many examples of the business activities that happened all around us that needed to be managed and caused noise (not necessarily music) that we had to dance through and around. I did my best to support all of the initiatives without losing sight of our priorities and keeping the team focused on our goals. We had a lot of work to do still and the implementation plans were well underway.

Shannon

With the budget process behind us and me back from a week of drinking amazing wine and eating way too much pasta and pizza (not really a thing), we could get back to work. While Kathy continued to remove roadblocks for us, the team needed to stay focused on the homework. We had made good progress, but we were just scratching the surface, and we needed to go faster. We also needed to sustain the new processes we were putting in place. It was time to implement layered process audits, to ensure that everything was working and, of course, to find improvement opportunities.

Even though our goal was for everyone involved knowing every process, it is difficult to keep track of so many continual changes. This led us to create visual work instructions to document the requirements of the new processes. We found that using pictures, arrows, and brief descriptions was much easier for training and auditing. Each owner was identified, and we trained everyone involved in the process, so they knew who was responsible for what. These visual work instructions were posted where the process occurred or at the machines. After the initial training, these weren't all that useful for the owner of the steps because they were living it every day. It was, however, useful for those of us auditing the processes.

Layered Process Audits

There are so many examples of layered process audits available, and they all work relatively the same way. As leaders, we wanted to be able to walk by the board that housed the output of the layered audits. As with all of the processes we implemented, we wanted to be able to quickly determine if there was an abnormal condition that needed to be addressed. One such abnormality in a layered process would be if a member of the team was noncompliant with their layer of the audit schedule. And guess what was posted on the board for anyone who wanted to know how the system worked?! Yep, visual work instructions. Layered process audits differ from a standard audit of a process because multiple people would be auditing the same process on the same day. I've found this confuses people and seems redundant to them, but the point is to drive accountability to do the audit and to help each other see. We structured the audits by week, so each person had a sheet they would populate throughout the week, checking one process per day. Then the "layer two" person would pull the "layer one" sheet and audit the same process. They would then review any discrepancies in their audit versus layer one with that person. They acted as a team that week. Once their audits were completed for the day, they would mark the calendar red or green. This visual control showed that they had completed the audit and whether they found an issue (red) or not (green). We would then record the issue found on an action tracker and assign names and dates to fix it. We added reviewing the action tracker and layered process audit board to our Daily Run-the-Business Meeting. That way, we could address the issues immediately to ensure they were resolved. Taking it to the next level, we added charts the teams would manually populate each time they found a discrepancy. This way, we could see where we struggled the most to comply with the process and dig into that area. This data also fed into our Daily Run-the-Business process observations we spoke of earlier by leading us to an area struggling and allowing us to review the issues as a team.

The audit questions were structured specifically to that process. You can make a more blanket approach and check the same thing for all processes; it just depends on your business. We would check things like 5S and standard work compliance, complete a time study, check for safety issues, material flow compliance, etc. After a few months of no significant findings, we would remove the process from the layered audit and add a new one. We found it important to keep the questions simple and the amount of time to complete an audit very reasonable. We went through a lot of trial and error to determine what was reasonable for us. It is easy to fall into the trap of "we need to audit everything," which could be true, but if it's not manageable, it becomes a check-the-box exercise, which serves no purpose. I've even taken this process out of plants where it was just that type of exercise, restructured it to check the meaningful few, and then reinstituted it. Just like anything else in this transformation process, try something and see what works and change what doesn't. I always told the team if this doesn't work, we will just change it! Nothing has to be permanent unless we decide it is. And for the sake of continuous improvement, most things should really never be permanent.

Besides looking for compliance in these audits, doing the standard work observations allowed the team to look for improvement opportunities and get one-on-one feedback from the operator on how things were going. We made sure to interact with the person working that process to inform them why we were there and what we were doing. Afterward, we would ask if they had anything on their minds that wasn't working well or could be improved. This is another way of engaging more people in the process and getting their input.

The more they are involved in how the process works, the more they will own it and want to improve it.

I will admit that I am not an audit person. I feel like this makes me vulnerable to admit as I know the value and great things that come from this process, and I have done my best to convince others of this. But I will say it anyway – it is a painful process for me. I will always do them because it's something I know is essential to the transformation process. (Just some days, it's a struggle!) It doesn't matter how far you are into your transformation journey; if you do not check what you have put in place over time, it will deteriorate. I have learned that the hard way when we've implemented a new process and assumed it was working fully, only to find out a month later it wasn't being followed at all. When such discoveries were made, we would question the operators as to why they weren't following it. Their answer was usually along the line, "it doesn't work the way you set it up." Frustration would follow. Writing this down now, it seems so easy – just put a layered process audit in, but it does take multiple tries to get it right for each business. As I mentioned, just start with anything that allows the teams to check what's been changed and continue to make improvements!

We continued to tap dance through the obstacles we would encounter and prepared ourselves to tackle the next phase in our journey. This would require us to put on yet a different type of shoe, one with a little less height, to accomplish what was ahead of us.

8

Flats – *Picking Up the Pace*

With two of the four plants solidly underway, we were starting to experience positive results. As we said, the first year was all about inputs without the outputs, so productivity was essentially flat as we were developing all these processes. However, at the beginning of the second year, we finally saw productivity start to increase. The divisional metrics showed that straight time hours were flat from the previous year, but we were producing 15% more parts with 19% less overtime. The process was working. Even though we were thrilled with these early results, we agreed we needed to pick up the pace. So, we decided to expand our endeavors and started tackling our third plant south of the border. Remember the early wardrobe decisions – flats versus heels? Well, flats are not quite as glamorous, but they do allow you to move faster!!

Sharing Expertise

Kathy

When you are a leader, you are asked to make presentations as though you are an expert in a subject area. You cannot delegate this responsibility because the presentation calls for a certain level of title to appeal to the intended audience. The worst is when you are in a setting where the presentation you have given is followed by a question and answer session and you are put in a position to answer questions where you know darned well that the audience knows you don't know the answer to their specific question, one that would have required you to work in their particular job for the better part of multiple decades. I have been put in that position too many times to count, and all I can say is, I choose one of two strategies when I don't know. I either honestly say that I don't know and I will get back to the person once I find out or I use my media training and just twist their question into some premeditated subliminal message I am trying to get across.

DOI: 10.4324/9781003196976-8

And so, approximately a year into this role, I was invited to Corporate to talk about how to grow sales to a group of senior engineering and marketing professionals. Our team had just won a prestigious internal award for an invention for the Oil & Gas market. The team at my division had been developing the material and design for years and just happened to win the award within my first year as leader. I was a bit uncomfortable being a part of accepting the award alongside my team because I believe that you must give credit where credit is due, and quite frankly, my predecessor was due the credit. He was the one who had allowed the team the time and energy to develop the innovative product. But, that's not how it goes; I was in the seat at the time, and so part of the "recognition" was providing a presentation on growth to other technical leaders in the company.

I searched my heart for the sweet spot, that place where I could be sincere in my presentation and not overstep my boundaries into our award-winner's technical aspects nor the great strategy I had developed that led us to this place. Instead, I talked about GROWTH from my perspective. I put together a presentation that outlined what I saw as areas that were going to help us grow our revenue in the future from lessons learned from this product and other successes I had seen around the company.

The GROWTH model I was endorsing was as follows:

> ***G****reat Products and Services*
> ***R****elationships*
> ***O****rganizational Design*
> ***W****ay Forward*
> ***T****eamwork*
> ***H****ealthy Environment*

As I look back on it now, I should have written a blog on this! If blogs had been invented at that time, I surely didn't know about them. I was able to talk about the product that had won the award and briefly discuss the philosophy we were using to provide space to create other innovations in products and services to continue our growth path. Developing relationships was a much more comfortable topic for me, so I discussed how we were starting to treat the inside sales team who brought us the opportunities as we would outside customers. I also discussed partnerships with universities and suppliers. We had done extensive work reorganizing the division to ensure that we had enough resources dedicated to innovation, separate from the large team of people servicing products we already had in the field. The way forward was the strategy deployment plan we developed. Teamwork was about how all the functions in the division are essential to successful growth. The healthy environment was based on the vision and values I led with and how we treated one another at the division. (Recall the discussion I had early on with my new team: no walls, no victim mentality, treat each other with dignity and respect, work hard, and have fun.)

I thought the reaction would be a bunch of eye-rolling; however, I received a lot of feedback from the audience that they had never considered such a comprehensive overview of all the components of growth. It was a great success. And it was 100% me, a much better approach than me trying to fake my way through a technical lecture.

On the Home Front

Emily had completed her first year of college – not without trials and tribulations. She had gone in with a roommate she had known from high school. That relationship went awry, and after many tearful phone calls late into the evening, they split into two rooms. It happens. As a mother, it was hard to watch her navigate through this. It was her learning to "adult" all on her own. The things I fantasized about that I could do to end the misery she was going through were not really socially acceptable. Ultimately, she resolved it on her own. I was just there to listen and support.

Claire had also successfully completed eighth grade, endearing many of her teaching teams through her sweet disposition and hard work. My living two hours from home for a good portion of the week was a challenge for all of us, and I was grateful for the school personnel who were always gracious recipients of my emails every week.

Sometimes, I felt like my husband was getting the short end of the stick with all I had on my plate. I put my heart and soul into my team and my job and made sure my children had everything they needed every day. If there were time and energy left, I shared it with my husband, who, after all, was an independent, self-sufficient human being. In my mind, he didn't need me as much as my team or my children. He was unbelievably patient with me and always my biggest supporter. One year into this assignment and with no end in sight to the dual-household arrangement, he sent me some pictures he knew I would like. I wrote back to him to thank him and let him know they made me smile. He answered, "Glad they make you smile, wish I could see your real smile. Love you!" I had a relationship worth investing in, and that gave me the energy I needed to keep pushing forward with acceleration.

Shannon was getting to know my family, which intersected with visits from Jeff, who would come up and work out of the lake house from time to time. That second summer, following my first full year in the job, everything was amped up a notch. I had hired three summer interns, all of whom I invited to live with me. Summers were so much fun at the lake with lots of visitors and less commuting back and forth as the girls could stay at the lake longer between school years. That summer, Shannon was in town a lot. She spent so much time with the young ladies, partaking in all kinds of activities with them. Monday night was reality show episodes and Tuesday nights were "ethnic food dinner night." There were movie nights (Magic Mike was a hit), celebrity gossip magazine reviews, and general girl talk about all things young ladies go through. It was a bit like a sorority house Shannon being the cool older sister figure, and me being the House-Mom (hoping that is the right term, as I had never been a sorority girl). To this day, Shannon remains in contact with each of those three young ladies who went on to have careers in Columbus, Chicago, and New York City. It was a lot of fun that summer – great memories made. Shannon was a fantastic role model to each of them, as she put her heart and soul into the work she was doing with the division. She was a great example of how hard work can lead you to successful places, and she was young enough that the girls could relate to her. We loved days when we wore matching company swag. I loved the days of coming home to a full house filled with youth and laughter.

Shannon That was such a fun and soul-lifting summer! The giggles, memories, and connections we made together made the long, challenging days much lighter.

Kathy *It was really fulfilling to see the young ladies get the opportunity to work in a place that gave them professional experience in a rugged environment. I watched their confidence build as they worked side-by-side with career professionals doing work that added value to the goals of the division.*

Developing Relationships

The relationships I was making with the other members of my team were blossoming as well and were helping us to move faster. There were challenges for sure. There were many different opinions and sometimes staff meetings had reverted to the storming phase, but we had a family-like way of working through issues. We were comfortable with debate, and many times, we were unable to reach a consensus on items, such as our particular product niche. However, when the debate ended, and a direction had to be forged, we left the room united. It was kind of like growing up with three brothers. They were constantly "challenging" each other with baseballs, wrestling, taunting, etc., but when a member outside of the family messed with any of them, they immediately became a united front. It didn't always work perfectly, and when it didn't, it was evident throughout the division. If it got unhealthy in terms of conflicting directions, I intervened. For the most part, we were like any other slightly dysfunctional family. Everyone had a voice. Nobody got their way all the time, and, at the end of the day, I was the leader, and it was my job to make sure this work-family of mine flourished.

I had a special relationship with each of them. They were all talented and caring people in their own ways. My Marketing Manager and I had very different demeanors, however. I am loud and demonstrative with my emotions, especially laughter, while he exuded calm with every fiber of his being. He was practical and knew his stuff. He had been in this business for a long time and was very effective at engaging me in customer issues that mattered. Otherwise, he handled the day-to-day. He often commented that he knew when I had arrived at my office each day, as he could hear me laugh before he saw me. He was a downtrodden Cleveland Browns fan. I was an enthusiastic Steeler fan. On the few occasions when my team struggled, he made sure it was included in a presentation he was giving or a roundtable item. I think his favorite time of every day was when I would walk by his office and tell him, "I have an idea." I believe his eye-rolling was really a form of admiration for the marketing ideas I would come up with.

Shannon See, I wasn't the only one doing the eye-rolling!

Kathy *I had a special relationship with my Human Resources Manager as well. He saw his job as partnering with me on strategic people issues and keeping me out of trouble, which I greatly appreciated. As an avid rule-follower, I was not that high risk, but he made my success his personal mission. That first summer with the interns, he wrote a memo to one of the girls, telling her to watch out for me during my birthday weekend. He said not to let me get out of control. He then retracted that sentiment and told her that she could, indeed, let me get out of control but had to make sure I wouldn't get caught. I am pretty sure she has not received many such emails from her other HR Managers in her career.*

My Materials Manager, Eric, who was always way ahead of the technology curve, asking for IT gadgets that were not available to the other workers (i-pads, etc.), was young and brilliant. He was before his time with the paperless movement and always had his nose down in his latest device during staff meetings. As this was a personal pet peeve of mine, I would often send him emails saying, "I see you." And he would answer, via email, that he was not doing email; he was just taking notes. I would shake my head at him but always let him continue, and it became our little joke. I did need him to have his head in the invention game lest I win my own innovative product award someday.

My IT Manager was so patient with my technical difficulties. (My husband called them PICNIC situations: "problem in chair, not in computer.") He would often tell me how he loved that his voice mattered under my administration, and he truly felt like a valued member of the leadership team. And he was!

My Controller worked as many hours as I did – partly because he would patiently go over the numbers with me again and again, as we tried to predict which monthly figure(s) would generate scrutiny or a multitude of detailed questions.

And my Supply Chain Manager was a seasoned professional that could always be counted on for a dose of sincerity and a hint of dry humor.

My Quality Manager used to be in the military Special Forces. Years before, he had literally gone into the jungle to bring home a very famous character that was prevalent in the news. A sniper bullet had grazed him. He only discussed those events in private conversation and when pressed to do so. He was unfazed by customer issues. He did not fear defects on parts. He had been through some real-life stuff, and he was a rock. I valued this so much as he would often remind me not to get worked up about the little things.

As I think back to this time with a year under my belt, it really is all about relationships. You have to develop them. You have to nurture them. You have to learn from others' relationships. You sometimes have to accept them for what they are or never will be. In retrospect, I believe the energy I was putting into these relationships helped drive the team toward new levels of performance.

Shannon

As you can tell, relationships were important to Kathy, and she put a lot of time and energy into getting to know everyone throughout the organization. As I learned early on, developing relationships was critical to my success; however, criticality was much larger in this role. I was still getting to know my peers and figuring out how to help them while pushing through some difficult changes. I was also getting to know every other level in the organization, and I worked hard to make sure they were all heard and that I had time to listen to them. In the office,

I kept working with the value stream transformations we were completing and kick-started new ones, but there were more layers to this process in the plant.

I've never felt that hierarchy mattered much. If you were the supervisor, group leader, or operator, you had an equally important voice. Each time I would sign a production status board, I would greet the operator and ask how they were and how things were going. If they gave me ideas or feedback, I would make sure to write it down. (Remember, I always had my notebook with me!) The key to this relationship-building was to ensure I followed up with each of them. Even if it were decided we weren't going to put their idea into action, I would let them know and explain why. This was challenging and time-consuming but very important. We were trying to develop a culture of engagement, but what would be the point of saying you want ideas if you weren't going to do anything with them?

Kathy *It's ok, Shannon, not all ideas are good ones.*

Shannon The great part was we were getting a lot of new ideas. The challenging part was trying to filter through all of them and continue to follow up. With this fast pace of change, I quickly had to learn how the team members dealt with change in the three different plants. I tailored my approach for each of them to get the best results. For example, I had one Quality Manager that required a little "seed planting." I would ask him his thoughts on how to change a particular process, listen to his ideas, share my own, and then sit on it for a bit. I'd then come back and start pushing the change that needed to take place. By then, he had time to think about, get comfortable with the fact that change was going to happen, and then became a champion of it.

Don't get me wrong; this is not about trickery. It's about understanding how people work differently and how to help make them comfortable with the idea of change. I would also ask for opinions, and team members would sway my original view with something better. This was the power of building trust and learning that each of us was willing to give at times to get better. And sometimes, I would simply say, "Here's what I want to do, and I have no idea how to do it. Do you have any ideas?" The bottom line is relationships are essential when going through a business transformation like this. It takes a lot of energy, effort, and stamina to care enough to build a culture of engagement where people want to change for the better. And it's much more successful and fulfilling than simply telling everyone what to do. Oh, and by the way, you may learn a thing or two (or hundreds) as I did.

Kathy *Anyone who has been a leader also knows how lonely the position can be. The responsibility for the business, the people, and their families' welfare lies with you. It was always important to have a peer, hopefully in another organization, that you could trust with your deep dark work secrets. No, nothing unethical, but things that frustrate you about the direction of certain policies, like dress codes, or layoffs, or having to make tough human resource decisions. This process may also include someone with whom you can blow steam off or share a laugh. You have to be careful choosing these people, as you don't want to scare or overwhelm them with your inner thoughts, but you do need a relationship with at least one of these people. I had one special person that I had worked on with many projects at Corporate. She and I developed a lot of programs together. She was smart and pure of heart. She coached me, acknowledged my accomplishments, and took the calls when I was distraught. One of the major qualifications she met to be a member of my circle of trust was that she found me amusing. We needed to have that in common. I try to find humor in things that are not consistent with how I view the world. Being able to joke about said items and move on with your life is one of my coping techniques.*

There were other peers I was able to turn to as well – ones that understood the struggle being real: the aggressive metrics, the frequent reviews, the hundreds of initiatives we were juggling. However, there were definitely some unique situations that a female senior manager had to learn to handle. There were not many of us around, so this was navigating new territory. One of these said items was the whole greeting situation. I am not sure where or when it happened, but somewhere along the way, many peers on my journey would hug or kiss me on the cheek as a greeting. It was all innocent enough, and I am a hugger, but I did not know who was in for the handshake versus who was in for the hug. My male counterparts never had to deal with such awkward situations, such as when you reach your hand out to shake another's hands, and they come in for a hug. You have to keep track of who is on the handshake versus the hug list. You also need to keep a list of all the countries you will visit for the one, two, or three cheek kiss customs and whether you need to start on the left or the right cheek, lest an awkward head bump or inadvertent lip meeting should occur. It's a lot of pressure to maneuver your arrival and departure at every meeting correctly. You want to be respected as a businessperson, but you don't want to appear to be aloof or stuck up, or unfriendly. At least I never did.

While I try to find some humor in these awkward situations, I promise you, it was accompanied by many hours of hard work, difficult initiatives, never-ending change management, prioritization, and conflict resolution. At the end of my first full fiscal year of serving as the General Manager, my boss asked me to provide a list of that year's accomplishments. Here is a sample of the list I submitted (with exact figures to back them up):

- *Shipped > 324 million parts @ > 95% on-time delivery*
- *Achieved double-digit rppm levels (no Quality Council invitations), record divisional performance*
- *Cost of Poor Quality best/lowest in past 10 years (gross scrap % of net sales)*
- *Record Return on Sales%*
- *Record Return on Net Assets*
- *Sales growth: 3%; transfer sales increased 35%*
- *Enabled New Business Awards with material technology advancements*
- *Established divisional safety council and plant safety councils*
- *31% reduction in recordable injuries through May*
- *50% reduction in Worker's Compensation cost/hour*

- *Achieved record Quote Win Rate of 43% in May*
- *Hired Division Lean Manager and Division Engineering Manager*
- *Sold millions in new product commercialization in new to world/new to market innovations*
- *Developed technology road map*
- *Developed APQP process, job requirements, and hired a coordinator*
- *Developed a business case for new products*
- *Recruited and hired three new engineers*
- *Instituted Problem-Solving Teams (pricing, premium freight reduction, turnover reduction, safety)*
- *Lean New Product Development Value Stream Transformation (viability/feasibility review, design standards)*
- *Implemented lean and continuous improvement methodology (EPEI, Standard Work, Operator Work Balance)*
- *Instituted many basic manufacturing tools: run the business meetings/day × hour boards, etc., layered audits)*
- *Created PFEP for two plants*
- *Created product/process matrix for three plants*
- *Completed Organization Design for growth: execution underway with Materials and Procurement Managers hired*
- *Hired three Market Managers for growth in target markets*
- *100% participation on Strategy Deployment teams for salaried workforce*
- *Major facility upgrades: painting/paneling removal: enabled customer classes to be held on-site*
- *Three product schools held (previously one/year)*
- *Major training investment/classes held @ various locations: Finance for Nonfinancial Managers, Lean Boot Camp II, OSHA Safety Training, Product Segmentation, Value Pricing*
- *#1 in Divisional Phantom Shopper Score*
- *Completed Test Lab Facility in Plant 1*
- *Coordinated many raw material shortage mitigation strategies for multiple peer divisions*
- *High-Performance Teams initiated in three plants*
- *Several IT systems implemented in support of the lean initiative*
- *Lot control system implemented in Plant 2 for quality improvements*
- *Formed two employee committees for charitable contributions and employee recognition*
- *Created quarterly divisional newsletter for employees*
- *Numerous compliments from Customers/Sales Organization; example: "Cleanest and most organized manufacturing facility seen in 27 years."*
- *Unsolicited employee feedback on cultural changes underway: "To be personally involved with the lean transformation and to see it actually working in our plant, to see the WIP stay down and the material flow through the plant has been both a privilege and a tremendous learning experience."*

My boss responded with "How about the top 5?" As a general rule of thumb, besides my brilliant marketing ideas (at least I thought they were brilliant), I was not one to toot my own horn or elaborate on my team's accomplishments. I always felt that philosophically it was better to keep my head down, work really hard, and let the results speak for themselves. The philosophy had always served me well until the previous year when I arrived at the division. I worked my tail off to keep the momentum going there, as half of the divisional staff had moved to another division, and made sure nothing fell through from my previous job as VP of Lean Enterprise and Quality for the entire corporation.

When I received my rating, I was given a "G" for good, or basically average performance. I couldn't believe it. The corporation's productivity and inventory numbers had never been better (listed in my goals). The division did not miss a beat, despite the change of leadership and half a staff. When I inquired about the rating, I was told that one of the leaders in my new chain of command had a policy that whenever someone was new to a job, a "G" was the highest rating he would allow. It didn't matter that I exceeded all of my goals nor that my previous boss rated me "exceptional" for my business skills. I was devastated. For me, I imagined that's what getting a lousy report card felt like. I wasn't so worried about the financial implications; if you were really good, you could maybe get a 3% raise; if you were bad, about a 1.8% raise. It was about recognition, arbitrary rules, and lack of process. The only way to seek justice was to go to my previous boss, who was my boss's boss's boss, and I knew the short-term resolution would only cause long-term pain for me.

So after the first full year in which my team covered so much ground, the comprehensive list I submitted was my little passive-aggressive way of saying that I am still going to hold my head high and rock this place, despite your underwhelming rating. I had resolved myself to never again care too much about these seemingly arbitrary rating schemes and just focus on providing a business that was healthy and able to support my employees and their families for generations to come. The transformation was more important than ever.

Expanding the Learnings

Shannon

With the process of transformations fresh in our minds and many lessons learned with the materials and equipment we were working with, we figured we could almost use a "plug and play" approach with our Mexico plant. We would find that the cultural differences would make it more challenging than expected, starting with the ever-changing and incredibly time-consuming border processes. This was where we learned to start and end our days in flats, as this was a highly unpredictable event that could take 15 minutes to an hour depending on the rules that day.

There was another unpredictable event that occurred once of picking up a hitchhiker at the border, one that the Plant Manager seemed to know. Kathy and I were asked to slide over to make room for our new amigo. This gentleman, who had placed his briefcase in the trunk, was an entirely unexpected addition to our trip and created quite the exchange of silent, yet meaningful, glances between us. It allowed us to practice our mind-reading skills. I said, "Who the Hell is this guy?" Kathy, without uttering a word, answered, "No idea, but not loving this situation right now." Me: "Should we say something?" Kathy: "I don't think so. I will handle this when we get to the plant." When we arrived, the stranger shook hands with our driver/Plant Manager, retrieved his briefcase from the trunk, and proceeded to take off down the street on foot. I am not sure exactly what was said during the brief exchange of actual spoken words Kathy and the Plant Manager had, but I think I did hear her exclaim something like, "Never in my life, did I think I would have to add 'No hitchhikers' to my list of safety rules!"

And, speaking of safety, there were the lunch hours, where our flat shoes came in handy. We would walk to the restaurant, dodging cars through multiple lanes of traffic, and trying not to get smashed, like a real-life game of Frogger. Every trip to Mexico contained some element of adventure.

In the plant was a fantastic group of people that created high-performing teams built on trust and camaraderie. It was energizing to be on the floor and see how happy the people were and how proud they were of the place they worked. They all had a handshake-type greeting that I loved since I'm a big fan of high fives. And, they excelled at working together to solve problems. We wanted to bottle up their energy and positivity and bring it back to the other plants. The facility was clean and orderly, and their performance metrics were relatively good. However, there was a lot of work-in-process inventory on the floor. There were some telltale signs of opportunity when you walked the floor and saw people chatting, not making parts with any sort of urgency – maybe a little extra staffing. I remembered a previous session with Rick Harris where he reminded us that "We hire people to work, not to do a job. All their wasted time is ours to get back." When I shared this with the team, it was not feedback that was well-received and recipients tended to get defensive. They were already successful with some of the best productivity rates in the division, but they could be so much better if they took this concept to heart.

Since Kathy and I are both relentless, we refused to give up and spent our days reviewing processes and setting up action plans to help the team understand what was truly needed. We lacked standard work and targets to tell us what was required to meet customer demand and hold people accountable. It was no different from the other plants but a very different culture, which led to a slightly different approach. At first, we received a lot of "Yes, we will do that" responses, but when we asked for follow-up evidence, it turned out they either didn't buy in or didn't understand what we were asking. This culture was more paternalistic, so if the leader wanted it to happen, it would. (In the United States, we had to convince everyone up and down the chain to embrace the changes.) I'm not sure which scenario was more difficult; it just required us to adapt to the different circumstances. This took us a while to figure out and admittedly slowed down progress. We eventually took them through a similar process, teaching the tools and engaging the operators. They excelled at continuous improvement and worked tirelessly to fine-tune their processes. Although their transformation was different, it still yielded great results.

Kathy *I had visited my Mexico team regularly to do production reviews and to spend time with the team there. They were a delightful bunch. I always took the leadership team, which was less than ten people, to dinner. We had rich discussions to get to know each other that would make us laugh, such as what is your favorite color? Where is your favorite place to vacation? If you could only choose one food to eat for the entire rest of your life, what would it be and why? What is your favorite song to be serenaded by a mariachi band? Things like that. We would giggle, and they would open up about their lives and ambitions. They were so generous with their time in the evenings. I loved going there to be with them.*

We would hold celebration meetings for all the employees during the days after touring the plant and attending all my scheduled calls with the teams back home. We would order special meals for all three shifts and I would serve the trays to all of the operators and the leadership team. I would give a small speech to them in gratitude for their hard work and their results. My three years of high school Spanish came in handy for these trips. However, I did practice my pronunciation with various people to make sure I wasn't inadvertently spewing cuss words. They were a wonderful, grateful group of people whose performance was the best in the division. They worked the transformation process, albeit a little differently, and their efforts drove them to an even higher level of performance.

Pushing Forward

Shannon We were spinning a lot of plates at once during this period, and once this team had their shoes embedded enough in the process, we let them run with it, with weekly/monthly check-ins, of course. We needed to shift focus back to the division headquarters as one high-volume-producing department had not embraced the journey yet and was falling significantly behind the rest of the plant. Although we mentioned that the pieces produced were starting to improve, we had a slight regression, and those metrics began to slip. Fortunately, we were able to home in on what was causing the problem and get that team on board. The new Plant Manager took ownership of getting it fixed and made sure there was accountability in that area.

It's not uncommon to have it seem that all the people are on board and saying the right things, yet one value stream/department/area is still struggling. In my experience, the main reason for this is the lack of buy-in or understanding from that frontline leader. Sometimes you can convert them, but sometimes you just can't, no matter how hard you try. My typical approach, and the one taken by the Plant Manager in this circumstance, was to break it down tactically. Find simple improvements that can have owners and due dates and see how that supervisor drives the improvement and accountability. These tasks included 5S because the area was a mess. They were not following the concept of "make a rule, follow a rule." We added extra help and attention from another supervisor and the lean engineer, removing all excuses to make progress. They continued with this approach for months and did make some progress, but it wasn't at the rate of the other value streams. It was bringing the plant and the overall morale of the team down. Therefore, a change needed to be made.

We continued to plug along through the summer and build stamina to survive the lack of air-conditioning in the plants. Besides being hot outside, we were running machines that were putting off 200 plus degrees of heat. Now that was a heat level I hadn't experienced, and our team members were troopers!

As we moved into our second Fall together, Kathy and I were finding our rhythm, but the team's progress was starting to stagnate. We were still completing our homework to the best of our ability, but we were simply plateauing, not reacting fast enough and fixing problems as they arose. Rick Harris noticed and reminded us that it is not always an upward trend of improvement during a transformation. Sometimes progress ebbs and flows. This journey has rough spots that you need to get through, but the sign of a good team is to push through it, "kick it into gear and move forward."

As I mentioned, we were using the tools, and the plant was starting to talk to us, but it wasn't enough. We were letting all the little things add up. By not addressing them, we were letting time and money slip away.

Our planning processes through Production Control were shaping up nicely. The material was starting to flow, velocity was increasing, the pull systems were working, and the pull boards looked good, but we were falling down in execution. If the boards were good, why did we still need to work overtime? We couldn't tell because day-by-hour boards were not updated with notes on why goals were missed. They were not being signed, and there were no consequences for not making the number. We were missing a sense of urgency. We populated the tools, but we weren't honest with ourselves on the actual performance, so the inputs to the tools were not correct, which was causing the system to fail. If we weren't capable of fixing this problem, we needed to be realistic with the numbers and change them, which would cause inventory to go up. We did not want that, but the system didn't work if our inputs weren't real.

We were even overproducing in some cases, which everyone seemed very pleased with, except Rick. How were we able to do that? And what impact did it have on all the upstream processes? What other process performance did we sacrifice because the one area overproduced? We didn't know the answers. So, how were we going to handle this differently? Production Control needed to control what parts to run and what overtime was required based on production rates. Manufacturing needed to execute the plan. I discussed early on that we made the switch to Production Control taking over the scheduling, but this was the next level. That department would manage all of the demand, set the targets, and dictate what overtime we would work. Talk about a major culture shift. The value stream managers would have to relinquish this control and truly have to start focusing on improving the processes and execution of the plan. With the roles and responsibilities clearly defined, it made hidden issues even more apparent.

We found we couldn't meet the schedule because people were not cross-trained on enough jobs, nor did we have the documentation to track this. We needed a training matrix and a plan to start training our operators, starting with critical processes that had to run no matter what. Our goal was to have at least three people per process/equipment fully trained. As we progressed through this, we learned that just training them wasn't enough; they had to practice regularly. So we set up "Backup Wednesdays," where the backup operator would run the process with the primary operator for a couple of hours, then by themselves for the rest. Yes, we were taking a productivity hit for having an extra person running the process for some time, but we were changing things so quickly, and this was our best option to ensure the backup person was fully up to speed. It was completely worth it because when the primary operator was off, the backup operator never missed a beat. The consequences to the backup operator not knowing how to do something was significantly worse than a few hours of productivity hit.

This was a tough Fall into Winter as we were still working through so many things to implement, improve, and fix. We trudged along, completing standard work, getting the data right, learning how to hold people accountable, and introducing more value streams. The list goes on. I'll be honest. It was a slow and painful time. We even reverted to the old cost-cutting pressures and end-of-year antics that historically ensued. This involved bleeding out every possible piece of inventory and not accepting material in when it was possible. We worked so hard to build our finished goods inventory to meet customer demand, and this was a major conflict of our strategy. Neither Kathy nor I had told the teams to do this, nor do we believe it is the right thing to do because inevitably, the next month, your customer delivery tanks and you spend extra money in overtime to build that inventory back up. The team ignored what our pull systems were telling them and what we knew was the right thing to do. We were frustrated that this had happened, but ultimately it is not abnormal for this type of old-school-organizational mentality to creep back in during this process. It was also an excellent lesson for the team to learn to trust the process and that we were serious about changing the way we do business.

As Kathy mentioned earlier, going through these lean or business transformations is not for the faint of heart, and this is precisely why. We could have easily given up at this point and called it good enough. We were a little discouraged after a couple of not-so-great visits with Rick and Kathy, but as Rick said, "the sign of a good team is to keep pushing forward." We were a great

> team, and we were determined not to stop, so that's what we did: put our heads down and kept doing the hard work (and occasionally wearing flats when it was needed). And hard work it was.

We were heading into a new year and another major presentation and tour that would showcase all of this hard work almost exactly one year after our team's debut.

9

Flip-Flops – *Not Your Typical Spring Break*

Life is full of special occasions. We look forward to them, plan for them, and celebrate them. We dress the part; we imbibe; we take part in the well-defined traditions. Sometimes these days turn out as well as we anticipated, and sometimes, not so much. Nevertheless, they are signposts of our memories, the days that mark something to look forward to between the routine days that fill the space in between. The start of this New Year was no different. The lean transformation had been underway for a year and a half. The time had come to host the Quarterly Lean Review – the one in which members of the C-suite left Corporate Headquarters and went to one of their plants to partake in reviews of the lean initiative for the company to see firsthand how it was taking hold in the field. This was a big occasion to look forward to and plan for. It was that moment of truth in which we would show the company's leaders that a team with the right leadership and culture can transform a business through the use of lean tools.

Special Occasions

Kathy

There were many other special occasions that occurred before the lean review would take place that year. Let's start with New Year's Eve. My husband and I took my in-laws out for a nice dinner downtown. We all dressed up to celebrate the arrival of another New Year, shared a special bottle of wine, reminisced about the previous year, and expressed our hopes for the upcoming year. We like to ring in a New Year at home, doing the countdown with the large, beautiful crystal ball that drops in Times Square. We toast with champagne, exchange kisses, and dance like the Rockettes to Frank Sinatra's "New York, New York!" We then call any of our daughters and parents who are not with us. It's low key, but it's our tradition, and we go to bed happy and optimistic about the next 365 days to come. Depending on what artists are rocking in the New Year on television, I will generally send texts

DOI: 10.4324/9781003196976-9

with my cartoon self-emoji wishing friends and team members a happy holiday. At 12:01 a.m., I grabbed my phone to start my celebratory texts and noticed I had an email from my boss. I remember thinking to myself how nice it was that he had sent me a message to wish me a Happy New Year. I opened the email to receive a message that asked for an update on year-end shipments. I guess, like last month's performance, the holiday had passed, and so it was on to the next task, all of 1 minute and 16 seconds into the New Year.

Then there were six weeks between New Year's and Valentine's Day. It was time to resume work on office 5S, office standard work, and material and information flow in the plants. There were Rick Harris visits and the homework reviews, price increases, customer visits, and the inter-company arguments over which method should be used to produce parts for windmills, oil and gas rigs, and automotive transmissions. I watched the lake turn from a large set of turbulent waves to a beautiful frozen sheet of glass in 24 hours. I spent a lot of time in my plants, sending pictures and love notes to my plant managers; things like "Who came up with this process of trimming parts with hand-held scissors and without cut-resistant gloves?" "Why are there three people doing it?" "Should we put up a day-by-hour board to measure the productivity of this optimal (not) process?" After walking the plants at times, I would send myself emails to remind me of things I spotted that needed to be followed up on. The subject line of those emails may have been entitled "ibuprofen refill needed," more than once.

Shannon I have to admit my heart sunk a little when I was the recipient of said emails!

Kathy *As frustrating as some of these observations were for me (and subsequently my Plant Manager), I had to admit that abnormal situations were quite obvious now. When I had first arrived, everything was in abnormal mode. Ibuprofen had been purchased in giant bottles from big box stores in those days. Now, when something outside of a defined standard was taking place, it was easy to spot and address. Yay, 5S and standard work! And, yay being able to purchase pain reliever in regular drug-store-sized bottles.*

The next occasion to look forward to (besides Office 5S and Pizza Day) was Valentine's Day. This year my husband and I planned to go to NYC for a fun romantic getaway and see a play or two. Since our careers kept us living in two different cities, we always made a special effort to enjoy our weekends together. It is not always easy to find jobs in the same locale when both of your jobs are leading manufacturing locations, and so it was out of necessity, not a choice, that we were earning the girls' tuition checks in two different areas of the state. I was really looking forward to our trip. My husband always sends me roses for special occasions. I was looking forward to being greeted at home with a vase full of red long stems. When I arrived, there were no such flowers. Instead, I received an email from my Marketing Manager with a picture of not one, but two dozen red roses that had been delivered to my office an hour after I left town. He let me know that he distributed them to all the ladies in the office since they would die before I planned to be back. I bit my lower lip, frustrated and a little sad; ok, maybe my spoiled self was a lot sad. Following this incident, an epic winter storm hit NYC, closing its airport and causing us to cancel our trip. I would like to say that I maturely handled the cancellation, but nothing could be further from the truth. Jeff eventually convinced me that we could still have a wonderful weekend at home. He planned a day for us at the local art museum and a fancy restaurant. As I was just starting to allow myself to feel better, the enjoyment I had been feeling from a nice day, great wine, and tasty pasta instantly vanished. It appeared that Justin Timberlake had made it into NYC to be the musical guest on Saturday Night Live. How bad could the weather really have been!?! When I arrived back at the office in the middle of the following week, there was a gift in the in-box on my desk – a little packet of flower food that had accompanied my roses. I will never know if it was just overlooked, or someone thought it was funny, but another memorable "special occasion" was in the books.

Shortly after Valentine's Day, we received word that due to some unforeseen circumstances at Corporate HQ, the date of the lean review at our division would have to be changed. The only time it could take place for our visitors was the first week of April. I replied that this would not work for our team, as it was Spring Break for the schools in our state, and many of us, both in leadership and on the shop floor, would be out of town, donning flip-flops and imbibing in adult beverages concocted in blenders, watching waves lap upon the beach. The response was that they were sorry, but the meeting had to be conducted that week. My team was not happy. Most canceled their vacation plans. I tried to convince my youngest daughter that a week at the lake with no sun and no boat would be just as fun as whatever southern US beach vacation we had planned to take.

Shannon This would be my first experience doing a tour this large. We had a lot of work to do to prepare, but we also had all of our homework to continue to work through, and I had to keep the team focused on pushing the change.

Kathy *So, we took to planning the visit, with meetings that revised the agenda, defined tour stops, and planned all the activities that could be accelerated to be complete in time for the big event. I must admit, we did fantasize about creating a Spring Break-themed review. We talked about ordering beach towels with the company logo, piping in Jimmy Buffet music in the overhead speakers we used to page people, and having cornhole and horseshoe tournament stops on the tour route. It was therapeutic.*

Shannon Therapeutic for sure, but I couldn't always tell when she was joking about such shenanigans!

Kathy *But, just like any special occasion, like graduation, a significant anniversary, or birthday, every detail was carefully planned out. Shannon kept the team focused, outlined the process for slide production, and worked with Corporate on finalizing an agenda. She kept helping the division aggressively transform to improved business performance. She was a true champion.*

We did have other special events in that first quarter as we were preparing for our Lean Spring Break Extravaganza. There was another lean review that was to take place at a sister division in another state. The divisional leaders (like me) were to bring their Lean Managers to tour the plant together and do our business reviews. When I forwarded the invitation to Shannon, her response consisted of two words: "road trip!" Clearly, this would not be a girl's trip where we could go shopping, wine tasting, or partake in other such fun activities, but we always looked forward to getting away as an opportunity to spend some quality time together. We would often stow away a bottle of red wine in one of our suitcases, and while the boys were out drinking beer in some hotel bar, we would pour our wine and engage in all sorts of topics that made us giggle. There were a cleaning crew or two across the country that were not too happy about these business trips, as red wine stains on white comforters are not that easy to clean.

Shannon We realize that not everyone has this type of relationship with their boss/subordinate, but that was just another special thing we shared. It takes a lot of trust to be able to completely be yourself without worrying about the work hierarchy!

Kathy *Travel can be a bit tricky for women. While nobody gives it a second thought for men to be sitting around in bars, drinking beer, or ordering shots for each other, if a woman partakes in such activities, it could damage her reputation, especially if she is the only female on the trip. There really are double standards one needs to be aware of.*

Shannon Sad, but so true! Your guard is always up in situations like this.

Kathy *On this trip, we were not so much concerned about our images but genuinely relieved to be in safe company with each other where we did not have to force conversations about topics we were not that interested in or had already lived through during the first 10 hours of fellowship during the day's meetings.*

On this road trip, we visited a division where my peer, who ran it, really despised me. He often called my boss to tell him things he was upset about my division for: lab charges, competing for books of business, and rent for the space my piece of large equipment occupied in his plant. I always asked my boss to have him call me first. My boss said he would. My peer never did. My boss did everything to remedy the situation between us, even making us have a lunch detention once where the three of us broke bread and tried to get us to resolve some of our issues amicably. Everyone else got to eat at the big table. When it was clear that I would not budge regarding my peer's Kindergarten-like behavior (I believe I used the word "tattle-tale"), my boss invited another of my peers to try to mediate. He got assigned to facilitate (referee) a workshop between our divisions. When the longest lunch ever finally ended and we were summoned back to the conference room, the drafted GM, who was walking with me back to the conference room, asked me why I couldn't be nice. I let out a hardy guffaw.

And so, it was, Shannon and I, on the road trip to my archnemesis' division, braced for the worst. Or at least I did. She thought I was just being a bit dramatic. After the "celebratory" group dinner and some forced small talk post-dessert, she and I got in the rental car. As soon as the doors latched behind us and our seat belts were buckled, she looked at me and said, "Wow, you weren't kidding. He really does hate you." Another loud guffaw followed by a great bottle of cabernet and in-depth analysis of everything everybody had said and done that day. Hey, it's cheaper than professional therapy.

Shannon We used to be amused at how differently we celebrated our holidays. Kathy and Jeff were great at celebrating all those mushy gushy holidays like Valentine's Day (and they are adorable doing it), where Scott and I choose to skip it. We both disliked the increased pressure to do something extraordinary to show how much we loved each other. Thank goodness this was mutual. St. Patrick's Day, however, we went all out. This is my favorite holiday of the year. Long gone were the days when I would take this day off work to head to downtown Chicago and celebrate in the numerous bars that provided that special green beer, but we still donned our green attire and managed to imbibe at home with a traditional corned beef dinner. At this point in our lives, special occasions weren't as marked by significant holidays as they were by work trips and weekends.

Kathy *While Shannon and Scott were enjoying their corned beef dinner, my St. Patrick's Day was a bit different. Again, not significant fanfare in our home, just an occasion to wear green and for my husband to have a beer on a weekday. And so, maybe we can attribute it to the luck of the Irish, but Jeff came to visit on this particular weeknight. After some benign evening activities, I went upstairs to retire for the evening. As I entered my bedroom, I felt something brush against my head and heard this projectile slam into the wall. I ran out of the room as though I was being chased by an axe murderer and screamed to Jeff the most terrifying words that have ever crossed my lips: "THERE'S A BAT IN OUR BEDROOM!!!!" "Are you sure?" "YES, I'M SURE! I ALMOST GOT BITTEN AND COULD HAVE DIED!!!"*

I immediately equipped him with an old tennis racket and sent him in. He could not find the bat at first, and I told him that I would never go in that room again until he provided evidence that the flying rodent had been removed from the premises. While Jeff searched our bedroom, I called animal control, numerous exterminators, and the police. I quickly ascertained that there is no professional available within 100 miles of our lake house to extract bats on an emergency basis.

Shannon Now do you see why I occasionally thought she was being dramatic?!?!

Kathy *I opened a bottle of wine and searched the internet for information about bats, shouting random facts to my husband as he continued to hunt down my predator. They were helpful tips such as, "If you find one bat, there is likely to be a whole colony of them in your house." I ordered a sound generator off Amazon that repels bats and probably a pair of shoes or two off the Nordstrom Rack website. It was a long night, but eventually, Jeff emerged victoriously. The bat had been detected and ejected from our balcony door. Calm was once again restored; however, I slept downstairs on a daybed and made Jeff cram in there with me for fear of other colonists making an appearance.*

How, you ask, does this relate to the luck of the Irish? Because Jeff would rarely have been there on a weeknight. If I had been there alone, my idea would have been to burn the place down. If Shannon had been there, although she is super brave with large bugs, I was not so sure that courage would exist with flying rodents. We probably would have snagged a bottle of wine and headed to a hotel, called a realtor the next morning, and never entered that home again.

Shannon She's right!

Kathy *Another nontraditional holiday memory was forever etched in our brains.*

Spring Break Lean Review

Finally, the next big occasion of the year arrived, Spring Break, or Corporate Lean Tour and Business Review Week. Preparation for this Spring Break Week did not involve donning flip-flops, the purchase of fun reading material, or the packing of SPF 50 suntan lotion. Instead, the preparation involved countless dry runs of slides and tours, a customized notebook for all visitors to take notes at tour stops, fun facts, and a quiz at the end of the day before the feedback session. Shannon will tell you about how much she loves fun facts. I will tell you they are necessary to keep a flock of visitors engaged in what you want them to focus on versus the myriad of abnormal situations that can arise between your last walkthrough and showtime. They are vital to a successful lean review.

Shannon Let me give a little more detail on the customized notebook – it had a plant layout with the tour route, value stream maps, pictures, and topics for each tour stop with space for the guest to take notes. It couldn't be stapled; it needed to be held together by a plastic spiral binder. No small feat to complete that!

Kathy *Totally worth it.*

Shannon We had over 120 action items to complete to prepare for the big event. We needed to make sure the boards were set up correctly, things were in the right place for the tour, boards purchased for our tour stops, cleanup was completed, lunch was ordered, and the list goes on. Every time Kathy got another "great idea," the list grew. (I say this with love because although her ideas were great, they generated more work!) I created an internal agenda with details on what every tour stop should cover, who would present, the amount of time at the stop, and even the amount of time to travel to each stop to ensure the tour did not go over our allotted time. Then there were the tour guide notes, which consisted of a script that prescribed word-for-word what the guides would say as they presented each tour stop. And, of course, let's not forget the fun facts to share while the group was moving.

Oh, the fun facts. I had spent hours and hours on this guide, making sure it would flow because the order would be different for each group. Then Kathy says, "You need to add fun facts," with me responding, "Are you serious?! What is a fun fact?" So much eye-rolling. I then spent time talking with my peers to come up with things to add to the tour. As annoying as this late request might have been (even though she was my boss, I was occasionally allowed to be annoyed!), Kathy was right about the fun facts. They are necessary to make sure the group focuses on you and not on the charts that may not be filled out correctly or inevitably wandering off and checking out things outside of the structured tour. No one wanted that.

Concurrent to all of that activity, I worked with every presenter to develop their board and practice, practice, and practice what they would say. Every minute of every hour of my day was filled with trying to work with the team. I did one-on-one practice sessions, then group dry runs, then dry runs with Kathy. Each time we took the feedback, made changes, and tried again. In addition to the tour, we had to prepare the presentation, which outlined our story and the results.

Kathy *The day of our lean tour could not have gone better. We greeted our guests with big smiles and leis, just kidding, no leis. We presented some pictures and metrics of the division before our lean transformation. This could possibly have involved a music video.*

Shannon Of course it did – this is Kathy we are talking about!

Kathy *We broke the group of visitors into small groups and led them through a series of presentations throughout our offices and manufacturing facility with military-like precision. All of the people who do the work were presenters. We wore matching shirts, along with a tour guide at the front and herder in the back (again, to prevent straying from the safe route). It was a proud day. It culminated in Shannon walking through a crisp presentation of the timing and key steps of our transformation process. We really had not presented it in such a systematic format before. Each step built on the prior, and the progression of metric improvement was captured and shared visually so that no results could be denied. The event ended with me doing a Question and Answer Session with our entire team and the visitors. Many questions were asked about lessons we learned along the way and pieces of advice we could give to other leaders and lean teams on the same journey.*

It was a huge success. My boss was proud, beaming ear to ear. His boss, too, was happy. My team was standing tall and confident, and maybe, just maybe, able to put thoughts about their cancelled vacations out of their minds for a few moments to bask in the positive feedback and palpable admiration of our guests.

Shannon There are so many details that go into these types of tours and presentations. There were matching shirts to choose, ensuring enough office space was available for visitors, setting up conference rooms, ordering a healthy lunch (lest the obesity crisis re-emerge), and booking a restaurant for dinner. Kathy was excellent at all of these details, and as much work as it added every time these "great ideas" would come up, they did add a level of specialness to our tour. Our lean review blew away the one we went to at her archnemesis's plant.

Kathy *A little competitive, are we?*

Shannon In fact, we were told it was the best lean review they had ever attended.

Kathy *Of course, it was!*

Shannon That was part of the two pages of feedback from 10 members of the visiting leadership team.

While this feedback felt really good and validated everything Kathy and I hoped to achieve for the team up to this point, the feedback that meant the most to me was what I received from our own team. There were emails of appreciation for our support and being given the ability to take ownership of the changes and improvements. There was also thanks for helping to make my peers and their teams look and feel good about what they do every day. I was truly humbled. We felt we had both proven ourselves finally and maybe gained a little breathing room to allow us to keep working and spend less time justifying. Things were changing, and now everyone could see and feel it. I was also relieved to have the tour over and get back to all the work we still had to do.

Kathy

This was it, my big goal of the year, from the very first moment of the year, literally, when asked about my shipments, I wanted to nail this visit. I had been told that NOBODY could ever become a VP of Operations until they had been a successful General Manager in the company first (a "rule" that would be broken for someone else shortly thereafter), and so, for the sake of my career, I had been driven to show them I could do it. Although, admittedly, this motivation to prove myself was secondary to my real passion of creating successful manufacturing operations. I wanted to create places where people could get good jobs to support their families. I wanted to create organizations in which people had the opportunity to contribute to the business in ways that they hadn't before. That was what was most fulfilling to me. But, I had fantasized about this being the day that my former boss, who had told me this "rule" so often, who was now my boss' boss' boss, would acknowledge that I was a good and successful leader.

And so, as he approached me after the crowd had dispersed, it was almost like slow motion. This was the moment I had known I was capable of all along, and now I would finally get the acknowledgment that I had convinced him as well. So, I smiled as he approached, and he looked at me and said, "Kathy, you have a lot of really smart women on your team. You are going to have to help get them moved into other divisions that need some diversity." That is what he said. Then he turned around and walked away.

And so, that Spring Break will not be remembered for sandy flip-flops, beach volleyball, sunsets on the water, or even half-priced aloe-vera bottles to take away the sting of a missed spot of lotion application. Instead, I will always remember that sting of an executive's diversity bonus where a dose of recognition should have been administered.

Shannon

Doing these types of tours may seem like extra non-value-added work. They take a lot of energy, organization, and teamwork to complete them successfully. However, if done correctly, they can actually accelerate the transformation. Receiving external recognition oftentimes builds trust within the team – trust in the process and trust in the leadership that has been asking them to try a radically different way of doing their work. These events should be planned with thoughtfulness, transparency, and the acknowledgment that we aren't perfect, but we are better than we've ever been.

We had a Rick Harris day the very next day, and we were all still riding high. Rick was proud of us, too. He recognized how important it was for the team to feel accomplished and for upper management to see the process at work and yielding significantly improved performance. But as Rick often did, he grounded us by reminding us that we should not bask in our glory too long, or "drink too much of our own Kool-Aid." We still had a long way to go. We laughed, agreed, and got back to work. Even though the Lean Review was over for most of the team, it wasn't quite over for Kathy. There were the post-review meetings scheduled the following day for the visitors. She was invited to participate.

The Flip-Flop Aftermath

Kathy

On the drive home from the Spring Break Lean Review, I cried. It was not the type of cry that is characterized by a few tears streaming gently down my cheeks, but the big ugly cry that is often accompanied by large gasps for air. It was a cry not only of a disappointment for unrealized affirmation but a cry of disbelief for such lack of empathy in my senior leader (and in my mind, probably all of humanity at that point). And, quite honestly, it was a cry which, for me, is always preceded by extreme exhaustion. My resilience is directly correlated to a steady dose of at least seven hours per night of uninterrupted sleep. I had not achieved that for many days leading up to the Spring Break Lean Review.

I grappled with my feelings and my extreme reaction to the comment about the females on my staff. Quite frankly, these comments were probably not that much more insensitive than many things said to me through the years. Besides the fact that my senior leader missed an opportunity to provide recognition and build a bond with me that I would cherish forever, I was insulted by the notion that my division was in some unusual location in which there is a disproportional number of smart women who were capable of being extraordinary leaders. I believe in choosing talent of all ages and gender, and nationalities. I choose the best person for the job regardless of what slice of the diversity pie chart they occupy. I feel that I attract a more diverse slate of candidates for my teams, but I would like to believe that it is because of how I lead, and how I include people, all people, in how I run my business.

The day after the review was tough for me. I was emotionally spent and felt so let down by what I had anticipated being a moment of reckoning, where I would finally be acknowledged as a transformative leader that got results through the methods the company endorsed. As I licked my wounds, I was keenly aware that everyone surrounding me was strutting around like proud peacocks. By all other accounts, the event had been an enormous success. My boss was thrilled. His boss was ecstatic. My team was deservedly proud, not only of the event but of the results they were getting. I held my disappointment to myself. I was so proud of my team.

That next day, I was asked to join the Corporate Lean Review that was being conducted in one of my conference rooms. I really did not want to join. In my heart of hearts, I just wanted all of the visitors to leave. I wanted to get back to my team and congratulate them on a job well done. I wanted to get on with business.

However, I accepted the invitation out of courtesy and compliance. You know how you can recall things so vividly, it's like you could recount every detail of the event? I remember where everyone was sitting in that conference room. I remember all the discussions. I remember biting my lip so hard during some of the conversations that were taking place that I was afraid I would draw blood. It was a best practice sharing and planning session. At that point, it felt like what I imagined being detained in a holding cell at the county jail might feel like. I needed to serve my sentence and repatriate into the real world.

One of the "best practice" sharing sessions was about recruiting people into the lean manufacturing jobs in the plant. One of my former team members from when I held the Corporate VP of Lean job offered the analogy that we wouldn't bring someone into the Finance Department without an accounting degree – why would we bring someone into the continuous improvement function without a formal education in lean methods? By the time this presentation was given, I had had enough. So, I raised my hand, reverting to the manners I had been taught as part of my Kindergarten experience, and offered a counterview. I started by taking a poll of my peers that were present. I asked them if any of them would take my Plant Lean Manager, who was brilliant the day before. All of them raised their hands. I then asked if any of them would take Shannon as their Division Lean Manager. They all raised their hands again. I then explained that neither of them had been trained at a University offering a lean curriculum. The Plant Lean Manager was a math major with a tremendous capacity to analyze, learn, and teach. I then recounted the argument I had with my previous manager telling me that Shannon was not qualified to be my Division Lean Manager for another similar, yet weak argument. I did not want to embarrass the presenter, but it was important for me to remind everyone that even though what we were doing in continuous improvement is important, it does not require formal education in the field. I feel strongly that it is essential to rotate smart people from all disciplines into these continuous improvement jobs to learn the methodologies, gain experience from implementation, become true believers, and then go back from whence they came, being evangelists of lean methods forever.

There were many nods acknowledging the points made during my monologue, and then a break was called.

As fate would have it, my phone rang during the break. My Mother-in-Law, who had come to stay with my daughter while I worked (did I mention it was Spring Break Week?), was on the other end. My Father-in-Law had fallen and split his head open, and they were on their way to the hospital in need of directions. I politely excused myself and headed toward home. Timing is everything.

As I reflect on this event, I am aware that I may still sound angry. I prefer to live in a world of positivity, fostering an inclusive and creative environment in the organizations I lead. Sometimes, it is hard for me to buffer my teams from external influences that are not similarly oriented. I still believe the world is generally good, and I loved my team – so it was time to pick myself up, brush myself off, and continue to lead. After all, there was a higher calling, a purpose, that was far more important than my personal career goals. I had benefitted so much in my life from manufacturing, and I am passionate that these jobs are an essential part of a healthy economy. People deserve to have the opportunity to have meaningful work and security in providing for their families. The best way to ensure the future is to create thriving and competitive businesses to employ the people you care about.

We had survived the Spring Break Tour, and even though we did not get a chance to wear our flip-flops that vacation season, it was a special occasion we wouldn't forget. Now we had to look forward, and up to additional hills we had to climb – hiking boots for the next leg of the journey.

10

Hiking Boots – *More Mountains to Climb*

One of the things that Rick would always tell us was that we would have to climb one mountain and reach the summit before we could see the next mountain that we needed to climb. So, here we were, gazing upon that next summit. We were coming to the close of our second year of transformation and while we had made significant improvements in material and information flow and our tugger routes were running regularly throughout our plants, we were starting to see that there were opportunities to improve material delivery even further. The manufacturing cells could also use an overhaul in ergonomics and methods that would increase output. Changeovers on equipment between product types were another productivity opportunity yet to be explored. Our ability to react to abnormal situations in a more efficient manner was also a goal for us. This would lead us to the introduction of Andon signals based on time-bound escalation plans. Andons are visual or audible signals that notify everyone that an abnormal condition has occurred. With the Spring Break Lean Review squarely behind us, all of these were in view on the horizon.

Unexpected Treasures

Kathy

During this time, other "you can't make this stuff up" moments were happening around the division. One fond memory occurred on a quality tour of another facility of mine, where I met the "Ghost Cat." Ghost Cat was a particularly scary large feline that had made its home among one of my older facilities, and I discovered it sitting on a box in the warehouse of incoming material. It was laying there staring me down, waving its tail back and forth, sensing my terror (I was

DOI: 10.4324/9781003196976-10

attacked by a cat as a small child and nearly lost an eye), almost daring for me to approach it. It was covered in gray soot, hence the name. I did a 180-degree turn and headed in the other direction to find the leader of the facility. My first set of inquiries with the leadership team in that plant came up empty. I was the only one who had ever seen the Ghost Cat, another reason the name was fitting. And, even after finding a paper plate with kitty food on it in the Supervisor's office, nobody could be entirely sure how that artifact had indeed found its way underneath that desk. Eventually, the mystery was solved after explaining on numerous occasions why a cat should not take up permanent residence in a manufacturing operation. Not sure the customers would appreciate it, and quite frankly, it was not the safest place for a member of the animal kingdom to flourish. Ghost Cat was relocated to a more appropriate domicile, and I added "animal control" to my list of General Manager responsibilities.

Shannon

I could not stop laughing when I heard Kathy talking about the need to get rid of this cat on a staff call. She found it less amusing though.

Kathy

As the end of the fiscal year arrived, it was time to submit our accomplishments which would be aggregated up throughout the company. I had learned in an earlier year that I could only provide three to five items, and that year, I was proud to submit these three:

- *3.5% organic growth (in a year when many divisions did not experience revenue increases)*
- *Continued team building/employee development (sincere notes from employees for opportunities to learn/contribute)*
- *Counter-cyclical business development by each business unit*

The days when it took every ounce of energy that my leadership team and I had to make our numbers had come to a minimum by implementing our lean operating system's processes, stabilizing the organization, and engaging everyone in solving problems. We were on to things that mattered for creating long-term sustainability. The energy was positive. We were on an upward trajectory.

I was feeling grateful. I had made real friends at Corporate from my days there. Over time, I had brought each of them in to help my team with different aspects of our strategic initiatives: cultivating virtues as a means of ensuring ethics and compliance, high-performance team development, sales growth through partnering with distributors. And I continued to communicate with those friends who would forward me the never-ending dress code memos distributed at headquarters. They were always good for a chuckle. Who would actually wear spandex to work? Were there really that many styles of capris that it was better to avoid them altogether? Ties for men were a definite HQ requirement, so I kept a plastic bag of them in my office closet for when some of my male colleagues would be summoned there for meetings. They complained the whole time leading up to such engagements, but I think they were secretly grateful that I cared about their basic workplace needs when I would whip out that bag of designer ties.

It was essential to keep a sense of humor when possible, to keep us "up" for union negotiations, monthly financial reviews, Tuesday morning weekly performance meetings, and the like. There was never a shortage of things that kept it real. We found comedic refuge in the language we had developed as a team, barely recognizable to an outsider. We held meetings in the "Super Secret Room" and giggled whenever we called meetings in this newfound productive piece of floor space.

We continued to work with Rick at three of our locations, combining his expertise in making material and information flow with the other aspects of the lean system toward new heights. I did vote with my calendar and did my best to spend the entire day with Rick, Shannon, and my teams whenever he visited.

That summer, as I was on my way to join the team in a Rick Harris day, my car died on the highway. I was able to get it to the side of the road (barely) and sat there in a torrential rainstorm in which I could not see more than two feet in front of the car. I put on my hazards and called for a tow, all the time praying that I would not be taken out by one of the semi's speeding by. Eventually, a police officer came by and asked me what the problem was. I told him my car had lost power and that I had coasted to the side of the road. He checked my license and asked me if I had run out of gas. I resisted the urge to roll my eyes at him but instead asked if he would stay there with his lights on to increase my visibility while I waited in the storm. He obliged (after he leaned in to look at my gas gauge, which was pegged to three-quarters of a tank).

Work travel is not glamorous, and it does not always go well. I must admit that I was nervous about sitting on the side of the road all alone. I felt vulnerable. I eventually made it to the plant after my car was towed to some remote town to a garage with no seats in the waiting room. A member of my team had come and driven me to the plant. I later learned it was his 60th birthday and will ever be eternally grateful for how he spent that milestone day. When I arrived at the plant, I joined Rick and Shannon on the floor and reviewed FIFO lanes and tried to put my car trauma behind me. My husband took over the car repair management, which involved a fuel sender unit, a jack, and an acetylene torch, which doesn't sound like the best repair equipment combination. Within a month, that car was sold and a newer vehicle was purchased. That was my idea of an irreversible corrective action.

My life became more intertwined with my nuclear family and my work family. I relied on my friends at work to help me through the garage door, sewer, and water problems, as I was still living remotely during some parts of every workweek. One of my business unit managers took my youngest daughter Claire and me on a fishing expedition on the lake as a little retreat from the online gym class she was taking that summer. We celebrated my other daughter Emily's 21st birthday with my team from work. She had been a returning summer student and grown fond of this work family of ours. Later that summer, Emily joined me on a field trip to Chicago as I was taking Claire to a One Direction concert. She stayed with Shannon and Scott while Claire and I went to the show of screaming teenage girls. Emily and Shannon had developed a little sister/big sister relationship. I was so grateful that Emily had someone I trusted to seek advice from on matters that moms really don't want to know about.

Shannon

I loved the relationships I'd developed with the girls, and that I could be a confidant for Emily. We had some fun, juicy talks that I would always keep between us!

Kathy

We had another weekend celebration for our staff and their spouses to continue to show appreciation for everyone's dedication, hard work, and results. The "Vegas Rules" protect some of the shenanigans associated with these adventures invoked during the weekend, but let's just say, a little fellowship, a little wine, a boat ride, maybe some dancing, and many laughs, the things of which memories are made. Good memories get you through difficult times. They also grow into legendary stories over time, stories that bond and unite, even stories that grow!

Unexpected Misfortune

Shannon

While summer was in full swing and the plants were trudging along in their boots, I was trying another pair of shoes – those of motherhood. Scott and I had been trying to start a family for quite some time, and I had finally gotten pregnant. We were so excited. We were also in the process of buying a new house – so many changes in my life both personally and professionally. I worked very hard to balance both and take care of myself and this little life I was growing. At the end of the first trimester, I went in for a routine doctor appointment. We couldn't hear the heartbeat. We had lost the baby. We were devastated. It was on the same day we learned this that Kathy was bringing Claire and Emily to our house. I had texted Kathy to inform her of the news so that she wouldn't be surprised when she arrived with the girls.

Kathy

I was heartbroken when I received Shannon's text. I knew how badly she had wanted that baby. As I drove, I debated in my mind whether I should tell the girls or not – and eventually decided that I needed to so they would know what had caused the deep sadness they would soon encounter. I searched my soul deeply. What words of comfort could I bring her? I was used to providing advice when she had frustrations or challenges at work – but this was a situation where there were no words that could take away the pain or diminish the loss. When I arrived at the house, Scott took the girls inside and Shannon came out on the front porch. I hugged her deeply. We then sat on the front stoop for a long time. I held her in my arms as she wept. I tried to hide the tears gently streaming down my face. I cried about her pain. I cried about the little one we would never meet and the dreams that had been crushed. I cried about what she would have to go through before she could put this behind her.

Shannon

When the tears eventually subsided and we went back into the house Kathy went to work on her phone, canceling my travel plans and the meetings I was scheduled to attend the following week.

I cried every day for weeks. I had never felt so alone in my entire life. My work suffered. I found it difficult to concentrate or find other tasks important. What did it all mean anymore?

It took many weeks, I think (honestly, I don't remember how long it was), many comforting and loving conversations with friends and family, and a night in the hot tub with Kathy and a couple of bottles of wine to move forward. But I did eventually find my strength, picked myself up, threw myself back into work, and tried again to add to our family.

Unfortunately, I know I'm not the first person who has suffered a miscarriage. I also know that there will be people in my life learning this about me for the first time. Why didn't I tell everyone? Would it have helped to have more people that care about me supporting me? Possibly. I kept this private for a couple of reasons. The first was because of this awful guilt I had that I had done something wrong. Regardless of what the doctors or anyone else told me, I went over and over in my head what I could have done wrong that caused this to happen. I felt like a failure. I also didn't want people talking about it like it was a topic worthy of gossip. I didn't think they would understand the pain I was in, and I didn't really want to talk about it. I'm sure these thoughts and feelings were a bit irrational, but that's just how it was for me. I was also incredibly fortunate to have a compassionate boss to see through my temporary setback in performance and passion for the job. I have no doubt many women suffer through this in silence, trying not to let the pain be seen and still perform at the same level. For that, and many other reasons, I am forever thankful that Kathy was in my life at that time.

Material Delivery and Ergonomic Improvements

Shannon — I climbed out of my personal valley of sadness to join the team again to conquer the next performance summit. The tools we had implemented were stable and the plant was "talking to us." The team's skills were really improving in understanding why we were doing the math and how all of the calculations supported the overall system we were creating. It was time to start looking at eliminating the next level of waste. Yes, we had invested in the tuggers to move material, but this next step was to determine how we would present the material during its delivery to our team members working in the manufacturing cells.

Kathy — *Tugger carts in a fabulous yellow!*

Shannon — We were still shy of our 20% productivity target. Using the operator balance charts and our observations during the Daily Run-the-Business meetings, we could see that there was more non-value-added activity to eliminate. We also identified many ergonomic issues that the current cell layouts were causing, both for the machine operators and for the tugger drivers delivering the material. We mentioned our commitment to keeping our people safe, and this was going to be our next opportunity for improvement. To work through how to make the improvements and keep the operators engaged, since they were the ones that would be impacted, we assembled a team of our operators, tugger drivers, and continuous improvement team members and conducted an event.

We found a space to work, measured the current footprint of each critical piece of the equipment and shelving, and created cardboard cutouts to see the full scale. We then set out to reduce bending and lifting and save time from cycle to cycle by eliminating the operator having to turn around to get materials. Another productivity gain we were targeting was rearranging how the machines were situated so we could enable our team members to run multiple machines versus being limited to one piece of equipment. We brainstormed many ideas and used our cardboard cutouts to evaluate each scenario. We had to ensure the flow racks weren't too high for either stakeholder and the machines could still be easily accessed for maintenance. The results were tremendous. We eliminated bending for the operator and tugger driver, reduced twisting from 180 degrees to 90 degrees or less, improved our cycles per hour, and freed up people to deploy elsewhere in the factory. The material was going to flow better. In addition to that, we had buy-in from our team members because they were involved and their voices heard.

Kathy *Their input mattered to us!*

Shannon Our hands got dirty (literally), and we bonded as a team, as everyone gained insight from each of the team member's unique perspectives.

With the concepts we generated in that event, we created a new plant layout. As the change throughout the facility was going to be quite extensive, we needed to get approval. Albeit a little slower than we preferred, we were able to acquire the funds we needed. Kathy always discouraged us from painting lines on the floor because, in a culture of continuous improvement, things change and evolve all the time. Nothing is set in stone. In this plant, blue aisles had been previously painted that were no longer going to be aisles with this layout change. Since we were spending money on the racking, we could not afford to replace the flooring at the same time, so we communicated with the plant on the upcoming changes and asked them to start to ignore the blue and begin following the newly taped aisles.

Kathy *See, don't use paint!*

Shannon A key to this was to communicate the multiple phases and timing of our layout implementation. We posted visuals everywhere. It was like creating a chess game where you strategically moved equipment one piece at a time. It would be ideal for getting the most frequently used equipment in place with the newly designed ergonomic setup. At times, the available floor space did not allow for that due to columns or other monuments, but we did the best we could to optimize the layout with the constraints we had.

As we changed the layout, another challenge we had was making freed up floor space usable. Small pockets of space only allow unwanted stuff to accumulate. We had spent so much time doing our 5S, and getting rid of unneeded stuff, that we didn't want to allow it to creep back in. We wanted to free up space to add more machines so we could grow, which required larger pockets to be created. As we freed up floor space, we blocked off the new area and made signs that said, "reserved for new business," which was great for customers to see when they visited our plants. Even in designing layouts, we were thinking of the customer.

The last part of the layout design was to make sure the material could easily flow. It was essential that the tugger could easily access the machines and navigate the aisles. We included the tugger drivers to help design the route. They were very familiar with the flow of the information and the material now, so they were the best people to make sure it would work smoothly. We learned a great lesson when we were determined to reduce the amount of walking they would have to do. We designed the route so that they were driving down the same aisle twice to deliver to each side of it. We had differences of opinions on whether this was the best approach or not, and finally, we just decided to ask the drivers what their preferences were in terms of ease. They said walking a few extra steps to deliver to both sides of the aisle was the best approach. Problem solved. As we progressed through the layout changes, we updated the standard work so the tugger drivers would know the interim steps, but in the end, we knew they would follow the standard work because they had created it!

Kathy *With yellow carts!*

Changeover Time Reduction

While we were steadily making productivity gains from our layout design, standard work, and operator balance chart actions, the next logical improvement involved changeovers. During our observations, Rick Harris would ask questions like, "How long does that machine sit there waiting for a changeover?" The answer was, "We don't know." "How long does the operator wait for material once the machine is changed over?" Lucky guess on the answer? "We don't know." "Ahhh, opportunity." Yes, there was a large opportunity to get this time back. We started tracking every changeover: start time, end time, who did the changeover. We learned that each person had varying times of completing the changeovers. We learned that more changeovers were done on certain shifts. And we learned that there was no standard. It was not acceptable that one person could do a changeover faster than another. They all needed to be held to the same standard. And that's where we started.

We observed each person doing the same changeover, asked them to document their steps, and got them together to review what should be the best process. Once we set the standard, we asked each of them to follow it. Then we set out to time each step, just like in any other piece of standard work we had created. We determined what was internal to the process (which had to be done during the setup) and what was external to the process (things that could be done before or after the setup). We moved as many steps as possible to external steps to reduce the amount of time the machine was down. Things like paperwork, gathering tools, and needed equipment would fall into this category. After we updated the standard work to include these improvements, we brainstormed how we could reduce the internal time.

We implemented ideas such as quick disconnects or longer gauges, so the operator didn't have to walk around the machine to check pressures. While none of this sounds like rocket science, it takes time and tenacity to break the cycle of "we've always done it this way." It was a lesson in patience for me and a lesson in authentic curiosity for the team to try something new. If you can persevere, you get better results. In some cases, we would classify the improvements as phenomenal results as we were able to reduce 70% of the changeover time. This directly translated to productivity since the machine was running that much longer.

Kathy *And, don't forget, it allowed us to produce smaller batch sizes since it wasn't such a big deal to change over anymore. This enabled great flexibility in terms of being able to produce what the customer wanted more closely.*

Shannon This work generated enthusiastic energy – and spread throughout our plants. Yes, each plant was filled with unique equipment, but the improvement methodology was the same, and the results were great!

Now that we knew what was going on in our changeover world, we could apply this to how much inventory we were holding.

Kathy *Math begets more math!*

Shannon We had to decide what we were willing to keep in inventory versus the cost of the changeover time. The faster the changeover, the more parts can be produced; less inventory is needed. And vice versa, as you drop inventory levels or EPEI (every part every interval: meaning you run smaller batches more often), it means more changeovers. So, in our never-ending strive for improvement, we decided to start tracking this to determine the impact. Using the math, we would trial this balance of inventory versus changeover. Ideally, we wanted to run parts for long enough to cover the changeover and do it strategically where we would run higher-volume parts more frequently and less of them and low-volume parts less frequently and more of them. We wanted to get good at the high-volume parts and subsequent changeovers first to get the biggest gains early on. We had ups and downs during this process. Still, ultimately as we got better and more consistent with the changeovers (and we knew we were because we were tracking them), we were able to bring inventory down substantially while keeping delivery up.

Andon Signals and Escalation Plans

One of the first and most powerful principles I had learned when I started in the role as the leader of the lean transformation was about visual controls. We had implemented so many of them on our journey so far. It was at this point that our thinking started to turn from the processes of producing parts to the process of making decisions. Were there different or additional visual controls that could help the leadership team accelerate reacting to abnormal situations? We turned to Andon systems and escalation plans.

There are so many options of Andon systems to help with visual controls, many of which are pricey. Frugality was still at play, even this far into our journey, so we had to find a very inexpensive way to help us see normal from abnormal. I don't remember exactly how the beverage (solo) cups came into play (I told you this was coming!).

Kathy *I guess there are numerous ways to generate creativity related to cups that most often contain adult beverages.*

Shannon We ended up using plastic pipes and plopped some different colored cups on them, and boom, super inexpensive visual controls in place. Red cups indicated that the manufacturing cell was behind their hourly production goals, green signaled that the cell was on track, and blue meant the cell wasn't scheduled to run that day. (The addition of the blue cup helped to see if the operator was missing from the cell or not.) When we did tours, people would always ask about the cups and why, and it was a simple response, "they are cheap, they don't break, and they are easy to change." And, of course, the color code was posted next to each cup so there would be no question about what they meant.

Implementation of our adult beverage color-coded cup Andon system led to escalation plans.

Kathy *Now there's a mouthful.*

Shannon The purpose of the escalation plans was to guide anyone walking by, taking note of a red cup/abnormal condition as to what actions to take. There was no more guesswork. Anyone could read it and know exactly what type of action to take. The steps in the escalation plan were time-bound – so as time went by without problem resolution, more resources were allocated to it. That way, whoever was checking the process knew who to go to and how much time to allow for the process to get back to normal (green cup placed at the end of the plastic pipe).

There is another process we learned so much from by letting it talk to us. Why were FIFO lanes backed up? Where did the process break down that allowed this to happen? How do we give something permission to arrive instead of pushing more material through the pipeline that can't be completed? These escalation plans were live documents that were continually updated as we watched how the processes were working. We kept getting better. With any Andon system or escalation plan, they are only as good as those responsible for using them. This took some effort, a lot of reminding, some frustration, and time to get this right. It required a high level of accountability up and down the hierarchy to make this work. We also ensured the cups were being utilized and actions were taken on issues through the layered process audit system we implemented. With these visual controls at each piece of equipment and process we'd put into place, we could walk the floor and gain a holistic view of what the factory was telling us. They also enabled us to make improvements faster.

Backsliding

While all of this sounds great, it was not always rainbows and unicorns. There were still rough points that we encountered. We were moving so fast and implementing so many changes, but we were not following up to ensure they were working as we had set them up. I remember a particularly difficult visit with Rick Harris, where we walked the floor and explained how these new processes worked, but as we stood and observed, what we saw happening was vastly different from what we had planned. We were putting the changes in but not checking them, and therefore they were not taking hold. It was frustrating because we had learned early on that if we don't audit, we will not be successful. We knew that but had overlooked it as part of this process. We knew better. The reality was, we went through multiple rough points throughout this journey, and this wouldn't be the last. Each time we learned something and had the opportunity to choose to improve.

As we traveled through all of these triumphs and challenges, our shoe styles continued to change with each one. The next pair we would need to try on would require heavy-duty strength. This part of our journey would require tenacity, courage, and the hearts and minds of all the people.

11

Combat Boots – *Battling for Lean Honor*

We had come such a long way and still had a long way to go, but it was starting to become evident that we had something really special that we were creating. The culture was inclusive and engaging. As we continued to expand our learnings and apply the implementation across every person, machine, job, and process, we learned of a new set of criteria that the Corporation was rolling out to identify lean model plants. We were going to use this opportunity to show that what we were doing was not only great, but we were creating one of the best plants in the company. Our people that had been working so hard deserved this recognition. Little would we know the battle we were signing ourselves up for.

Lofty Goals

Kathy *If I could characterize the next number of months, I would use the word "resilience." It was at this point that the company announced an initiative in which it would support the development of lean model plants. To be recognized as a model, the plant had to earn a certain score of tool adoption on a lean assessment and specific levels of improvement in key performance metrics, including quality, delivery,*

DOI: 10.4324/9781003196976-11

and productivity. This initiative would drive business results in the "right" way and create locations that could serve as places of learning for leaders and employees from other parts of the company. It was about accelerating lean implementation across the Corporation. I wholeheartedly supported it. Most of the basics had been put in place across the 300 plus plants in the company. Still, a few facilities would become elite examples of how to take the concepts and run by this lean operating system in all aspects of their business. I was all in. And none of my plants were chosen to be a part of the model plant process. The reason was that my plants were not among the largest in our product line. It made sense that the plants that generated the most revenue were chosen first to gain the most positive impact for the company. I supported that rationale completely.

However, for those of you who are operations professionals, you know that cannot be the end of the story. We are a certain breed. We are competitive, and we don't like to lose. Our lives are categorized as green/red, win/loss, and good/bad based on the numbers we make every day. I was not going to be left out of this competition. So, I chose to get us in the game. No, we were not drafted players, but we were going to be formidable walk-on athletes.

Shannon Remember when I mentioned that we really like competition!?!

Kathy *I chose a different plant from the one we showcased during the Spring Break-No-Flip-Flops-Lean Review to enter this competition. Two reasons: one, it was my biggest plant, so it would have the biggest impact on my business results. Second, the first plant would continue to develop, and people would perceive it to have had a head start.*

Shannon and Team accepted the challenge. All motivated by the many improvements they'd made and the numbers proving out, they were ready to go. This was not going to be a sprint, but truly a marathon, as to achieve model status, there was an element of the processes and results achieving a certain level of sustainability, and rightly so. That just takes time. And perseverance, and did I mention resilience??

Although this was Shannon's full-time job, for me, it was a fraction of what I could support with my calendar. I was still shipping parts and carrying out all the growth, human resources, supply chain, and all the other functional initiatives. And, of course, there was life to be lived along the way by all of us.

Meanwhile, Shannon was all over the new goal. She was taking charge of the transformation, engaging everyone in the transition. I have always admired her organizational skills. There was nowhere to hide if you had signed up for a task and a due date when you had someone who was a knowledgeable program manager. And the best part of all was I had really seen her grow. She used to get so frustrated when people didn't get their work done. Over time, she still held herself and the team accountable but became more of a teacher and coach. The team had come to trust her, really trust her, and it warmed my heart to watch as people sought her out for advice and counsel.

Opportunities Everywhere

Kathy

In the Fall, the Plant Manager position became open at our aspiring model plant, the one that was Shannon's home base. The Plant Manager role is critical in any operation and crucial in terms of the success of the implementation of any lean system. I felt that Shannon was ready for such a position. It was the right time and opportunity for her professional development.

At first, she was not interested. The Plant Manager reported to the Business Unit Manager, which meant that she would no longer have a place on my staff. She also was not interested in moving from her current position until we had attained the model plant Certification. She wanted to finish the job. If she took the Plant Manager role, who would take her place to help the plant with implementing the rest of the feedback? After many long and arduous discussions (much more challenging during the workday and without champagne flutes), she agreed to take the job. It is tough to take a step backward or sideways when you are used to an upward career trajectory, but there are times it is the right thing to do to obtain experiences that will serve you well in the long run. I have been there myself. It is difficult on the ego.

Shannon

I wasn't ready to leave my current role and take on something new. I wanted to finish this job, and I was really hitting my stride in it. I was enjoying working with the teams and learning so much about the business. Not to mention the amount of opportunity there was for me to help. I would be giving up working on the other three plants and take on responsibility for running the day-to-day operation of one of them. Not reporting to Kathy any longer was a tough pill to swallow. I was taking a step back to get valuable experience that I knew I needed to prepare me for more opportunities with greater responsibility in the future. There is also something to be said about being able to come home every night. This job would get me off the road and do just that. Another positive, from my perspective, was the plant I would be running would also be the one pushing for model plant certification, and I would get to own that. After many conversations with multiple people in my life, I decided to take it on. It was my first job where I would have direct responsibility for profitability, and I needed to be able to walk the talk and own it, versus being a teacher to these teams. So, I said my goodbyes to the other three plants and reluctantly handed over the reins. I took everything I'd learned from that role and jumped with both feet into my new challenge of running the operation.

And as fate would have it, not long after accepting my new job, I learned that I was pregnant again. This time I would get my chance to have a healthy baby. So, I spent the next several months being more tired than I've ever been and suffered through what felt like a never-ending hangover every single day. I would have my crackers and water with some type of fruit in it on my desk all day long (because water alone made me want to throw up), trying to get through each day. I wanted to wait past the first trimester to tell anyone, so keeping the secret became another energy-sucking exercise. Oh, and be a leader to hundreds of people, continue the transformation, and work through the model plant battle. Talk about juggling work and life! The days were long, but the time went fast.

Kathy *We continued to work hard to implement our lean system, taking us to new performance levels. There were times when there were two steps forward and one step back. I would get so frustrated when areas of the plant would regress, but it is a part of the learning process. I had to remind myself of that while still pushing the team forward with varying motivational methods and words. In one of my notes to Shannon in the Fall of that year, I advised, "When you meet with the team on the plan, remind them it's not so much about the plan, but the execution of the plan and just some manufacturing discipline/basics."*

Shannon That was a fun email to receive!

Kathy *This was a time of frustration at some of the observations I was making on the floor. And, admittedly, there were many other times when my messaging was less challenging and more affirming, all smiles accompanied by handshakes, hugs, and some "you rock!" or "you got this!" I tried to emote positive energy, and I certainly relished when I could absorb some of that energy back from the troops.*

I expended just as much emotion and energy in my personal life. On weekends, we would go to the various Big-10 schools our daughters attended to tailgate and watch football. One of the leaders of a distributor (customer) of mine had a son on the Indiana University football team. We had a lot of fun celebrating football weekends with his family, who considered pre-game festivities to be on the same order of magnitude as some weddings I have attended.

This was also during the first year of Claire's instruction toward making her Confirmation. Her program involved several religious retreats, and I was aware that she would be one of the few teenagers who had not gone to Catholic High School. I was worried about her not having any friends at the first retreat. I called the leaders and asked if I could volunteer on the weekend to make sure she would be ok. They told me that, yes, they did indeed need help in the kitchen; so, I immediately signed up. As a person who does not cook, ever, that weekend was character building.

Shannon I believe when I heard this plan I said, "Are you crazy?! Then I laughed at the visual in my head of Kathy in the kitchen cooking for all of these kids. I could not wait to hear how it went!

Kathy *There were a lot of teenagers, dishes, meals, snacks (which I did not feel were particularly needed due to my concern about obesity in youth – or possibly just a need to get off my feet), and encounters with Claire where she was begging me to take her home. We persisted, and even though I told her not to call me "Mom" in front of the priest after she had told him I had not taken her to Confession since second grade, we did survive the weekend. On Saturday afternoon, I called Emily and tried to make her feel guilty for not joining us in this noble volunteering activity. Ever the one with sharp comebacks, she told me she would love to be there. Still, she was busy entertaining my distributor customer friend at an epic tailgate party.*

Cultivating customer relationships and making sales for me was probably a more supportive activity concerning my life's goals. That perspective was a bit difficult for me to argue with.

Back at the division, we were starting to feel confident that we were approaching a level of maturity in which a first audit for model plant status was appropriate. Shannon was putting together an evidence book, which is exactly what it sounds like. For every category in the lean criteria assessment, she had photos of how we had implemented the defined tool/concept in multiple areas of the operation. The key performance metrics were indicative of a significant trend in the positive direction. We were starting to get excited.

Before we would get to that first audit, we had another tradition to celebrate that we had come to treasure – our annual Christmas party. This year was no exception. Scott and Shannon drove down from Chicago to stay with us at the lake. When Shannon arrived, she had brought several wine bottles – which is a custom we had adopted early on for visits we made to each other's homes. She showed me a bottle of wine, and I noticed that it was a non-alcoholic wine. I didn't know that was a thing. I thought it was an odd choice to bring for a holiday party, but whatever. We had shared enough discussions in the hot tub (inspired by a bottle of bubbly or two) for me to know that she did enjoy a cocktail with which to celebrate or contemplate life or the proper way to do value stream maps of office processes. She said that she needed to bring it to the party so nobody would be suspicious. Suspicious of what!?! And then it dawned on me; she was letting me know that she was pregnant!! We shrieked and hugged. I was so thrilled for her! And it was great that we had a designated driver for the evening as well!

Shortly after that, we welcomed the New Year. Jeff's alma mater, Michigan State, was going to the Rose Bowl, and as a result, so were we. To this day, I have no idea what we paid for those tickets (but I do think I could have an entire closet full of designer stilettos for the equivalency). Off to Pasadena, we went with two of our daughters, the two who had displayed some Sparty Football enthusiasm through the years. It took me a while to adopt the "Go White" response to the "Go Green" greeting we received every two seconds, but when I mastered it, I must admit it was much less awkward than when I would respond: "thank you?" With a green/white victory to start the New Year, I couldn't help but be excited about other events to come. Personally, we were getting a new baby, and professionally we would also be celebrating being one of the first model plants in the whole company.

The Season of Model Plant Audits

Our first audit was to be in February. Shannon submitted the evidence book and booked time for the review. It was painful. Really painful. Shannon kept a stiff upper lip and wrote down the feedback, all 300 items of it. Some of it was valid and constructive; some of it was a bit less than helpful. However, we smiled, thanked the Corporate Lean Leader (a.k.a. my successor and close friend) for the feedback, and told him we would be back in touch when we had addressed the items he had pointed out.

The team was a bit deflated, but I knew it was a part of the process and encouraged the team to get back to work on our goal for the year. They say, "That which doesn't kill you makes you stronger." In all fairness, it was a very responsible thing for the auditor to do to provide us with critical feedback. Not only was it in the spirit of truly making us better, but neither he nor I wanted to open ourselves up for criticism regarding any level of favoritism.

Shannon

It was a good thing we were building such a close-knit team because we needed each other for support when it came time for our first model plant audit. Kathy used the word "painful." I'd call it "brutal." We had been working for months on the actions, and we felt good about our progress and the evidence we had to support it. The Auditor, however, didn't have the same perspective. We took the feedback. We were still in the "you can't stop us" phase of our mission. So, we added the additional tasks to our list, knowing that the next audit would mean we had made it.

Kathy

After a couple of months, Shannon had led the team through the 300 and some odd tasks, and our evidence book grew with pictures and data proving our success; we invited the Corporate Lean team back for our second audit. We had expected that by completing everything from the first audit, this would be it! Unfortunately, the day did not go that way and a new set of criteria to become certified was established. Now you had to attain certification on the separate Quality Assessment as well. Being that this was a plant that primarily served the automotive market, quality was in good shape. However, one of the requirements was that your Divisional Quality Leader had to have a Black Belt for you to qualify. Had this been the original criteria, we would have initiated that much earlier in the process, but this was a new hurdle we had to jump over. We were justifiably upset by changing the finish line so close to achieving it. Additionally, although we closed out all of the earlier pieces of feedback, the audit delivered even more actions. It was very frustrating. This new list of improvement opportunities was dubbed "The Matching Magnet" list. One piece of feedback we were given was that we had to have the same magnets on all of our visual display boards throughout the plant. I believe he just wanted us to look professional, as certification would surely bring in many visitors. But this really deflated the team. They felt that the whole process was fraught with roadblocks.

We went to the local dollar store, bought the magnets, and distributed them to all the visual boards throughout the plant. We were consumed with achieving our goal.

Shannon

With the criteria seeming to change continuously, these new requirements started to feel unachievable, but we were determined to win this game. So, we kept our heads down and completed this second list of tasks.

We were on to our third in-person audit. Again, receiving more feedback, sometimes conflicting from the previous audits and what was perceived by the team to be an ever-moving target. I had kept it together for months, pushing through these actions, some of which we thought were completely non-value-added, and at this point, I was done. I cried the whole way home at the end of the audit day. (Remember I was pregnant!) I didn't know how to approach the team the next day. I didn't want them to know how upset I was, although I'm pretty sure my face that entire day gave it away. I felt like I'd failed them.

We met as a team the next day to discuss how we would tackle these new requirements. The team was down, and we agreed to make it a safe space to speak freely. The team shared their frustrations about how ridiculous this process had become. How could matching magnets help the customer? How many more graphs needed to be formatted in different ways to show the same results? We felt that we had done everything right to improve the business, help the customer and the company, and had the improved metrics to prove it. Not that we believed we had arrived, achieved, or were done with our journey, but the latest round of actions for this certification wasn't doing any of the things we thought were valuable. The team asked if we could stop the nonsense and get back to focusing on our lean transformation and the things that would actually help the business. We would still like to get the certification, but we wanted to pause for a bit. I didn't know what to say except that I would propose it to Kathy.

Kathy

Shannon was six months pregnant and had so been looking forward to wrapping up this achievement before she would embark on the event that would forever change her life. Tensions were high. I will never forget the call I got from Shannon. From the other end of the phone, she was telling me that the team at the plant was as committed as ever to achieving model plant status, but they needed a break and wanted to work on things that would improve the business for a while. They would look into resuming this certification process sometime in the Fall. I can picture exactly where I was sitting when that call came in. I told her I would consider the team's recommendation.

When I hung up the phone, I sat there in silence. I pride myself on taking input from the team, but we were so close to the finish line, and I did not want us to give up. What was most disturbing to me was that the team had disassociated their lean implementation with things that are focused on the business through this certification process. How had this happened? Had I let what should have been a good goal pass the limits of sensibility? This was one of those times when leadership was a very lonely place. I wasn't sure what to do. If I consulted with anyone else on my team, I would have to take their viewpoints into consideration. This was a debate I needed to settle within myself.

I slept on it.

When I woke up the next day, I called my boss. I told him I had made a decision and that I hoped he would be supportive. I told him about the request from my team. I explained the process we had gone through. With all good intentions from everyone's perspective, it had become one of those initiatives that had taken on a life of its own when internal priorities blind us from our primary purpose of serving our customers. And while the team was still doing an excellent job with quality and delivery, we had lost their hearts on their primary daily purpose of optimizing the business to provide the very best value for our customers. We needed to get back to that, and it would have been a real tragedy had the team forever separated this lean initiative and providing value to those we served. We needed a punctuation mark for our efforts.

I did not want to alienate my colleagues at Corporate, but it was time to end this madness.

Shannon

Kathy did not want us to quit for many reasons. The biggest being they were going to change the criteria formally within the next few months, and the auditing cycle would have to start over. Honestly, we were so burnt out trying to achieve this pie in the sky certification; we didn't care. The process had gotten so out of control. I disagreed with continuing, but Kathy was adamant that we do so. I understood her reasons and eventually put a smile on my face and rallied the team. I explained the reasons and told them I truly believed we could do this. Kathy was also going to send people from her other plants to help complete our action items. After some grumbling, we laced up our combat boots and continued the battle.

While all of this was going on at work, I started to experience some serious complications in my pregnancy. The doctor put me on bed rest. I was not allowed to go to work. I had to minimize walking and sitting upright. I had to do everything I could to keep the baby inside as long as possible because it was too early for him to join the world. Thank goodness for our incredibly tight team because I was able to work from home through the rest of the certification. Our Production Control Manager, a.k.a. "Other Rick" ran the plant for me, with me, through our remote communications. I had calls scheduled multiple times a day with my Supervisors, "Other Rick," and my HR partner, "Other Kathy," who had also become a close friend and supporter. They were truly there for me and our mission every step of the way. I kept working on building more evidence in the book, and the team would send pictures from the plant to support it. I just wanted this to be done before I had the baby, and time was ticking away quickly. We had become like a family, as often happens when people are going through something as big as we were, and I think they wanted this for me as well. I could not have been luckier to have so much support.

Kathy

While the team kept pushing through the model plant tasks, they were also taking the plant to the next level in terms of performance. I knew the team was ready and would achieve all of the goals laid out for them, so I set up the lean celebration for July. I told our Corporate Lean representative that he could have conference calls with us twice a week to help guide us through the remaining pieces of feedback. If we resolved his concerns by the time of the lean tour/celebration and wanted to award us with model plant status, then so be it. If not, we were going to celebrate our lean transformation without holding that certification. In my mind, and with the level of knowledge I had, having led dozens of plants to a model status (including one Shingo Award), we had achieved our goal. Our costs were down significantly. Our delivery was up; our quality was better; our inventory was much lower. Our productivity was at unprecedented levels in the plant's history. Everyone was included and contributed to getting us there. It was time to recognize the accomplishment and move on to doing what we did best: serving our customers.

I had the banners, the T-shirts, and the refreshments ordered and started crafting the music videos. We would share our journey with our guests: other divisional leaders and members of the extended leadership team, and the Corporate lean people. We were going to say thank you to everyone in the plant. We were going to pause and reflect on how far we had come, and I was going to use some of the cost savings to air-condition the plant. It was the best way I could think of to express gratitude to my team. And after all, weren't we doing all of this for them in the end anyway?

Shannon

Kathy told us about the celebration we would be having in July, a month before the baby was due. I don't remember her telling us that we would be having the celebration even if we didn't get final approval on the certification, however. I think part of it was that she had confidence in us that we could achieve it, and the other part was showing that no amount of mismatched magnets could take away the results we had. As I'm sure you've gathered by now, Kathy knows how to host a celebration! But, what I would learn is that before I could put on my party shoes, I'd have to gather a ton of data and suppress my eye-rolling (even though I was by myself at home, she could somehow feel them) to get ready for this epic acknowledgment of our achievements.

12

Party Shoes – *Time to Celebrate*

It was time! We had finally been recognized for achieving model plant status. We were able to try on our final pair of shoes to celebrate. Even though party shoes were in order, our lean transformation was not over, as it should never be in the culture of continuous improvement that had come to characterize our plant. Of course, we wouldn't retire all of our different types of shoes because, in any journey, there are times when you need to go back to tap dancing, being the sheriff, or even going to battle. And we would continue to do so, but for now, we would party!

Kathy

Sometime between when I declared victory and the epic lean celebration that happened on July 7th, we were granted model plant status. I have to admit that the letter acknowledging the attainment of the recognition was a bit anticlimactic after all of the struggles to get there. Shannon had been placed on bed rest in early June, which added a wrinkle to the whole process. I could not throw the party without her. Nor could I cancel the celebration. I had way too many plans in place by this point. I rented a wheelchair to transport her around for the day. I advised her that she needed to just go along with all of the things planned for the day. Never one to cooperate, at least without an eye roll or two, she was a bit concerned about what I had in store for her that day.

DOI: 10.4324/9781003196976-12

Shannon

I knew Kathy was up to all kinds of party planning antics when she requested pictures of everyone in the plant and mounds upon mounds of data. Although the data request wasn't specific, I spent hours putting together every piece of important statistic I could think of that would show trends of improvement. I double-checked every chart I sent because what the data showed was almost too good to believe. (It really was that good, by the way!)

The day had finally arrived to celebrate, and I headed back into the plant a little blind. I had gone through the tour extensively with the team over the phone and asked them to complete many dry runs. They had also sent pictures of their boards, which we discussed and practiced rehearsing, again over the phone. I'll admit I was a little nervous about how it was going to go, but in the grand scheme of what I was going through with the pregnancy, we had already achieved what we set out to, and I knew the team was going to do great. (Talk about a major shift in priorities for me and actually giving up control! Yay for personal growth!)

When I arrived, there was a wheelchair waiting for me. They had prepped me for this, but I didn't think it was really going to be there. I should be grateful it wasn't one of those motorized wheelchairs they threatened me with. When Kathy advised me that I needed to "just go with it" for the day's events, I hesitated with my reply, stating that I was not going to sing. Fortunately, for everyone else's sake, this was not a request that was made.

Kathy

We started with lunch and a presentation. My peers were all there to celebrate with us, as well as my boss and his staff. I bought everyone matching shirts, and they all were very supportive and put them on to celebrate with the team. I wheeled Shannon into a conference room, where we held a meeting to explain the process we went through to attain model plant status. And, of course, it started with a music video. It had a lot of the statistics associated with the audit process to become a model plant. It also had numerous pictures of Shannon in the plant with the auditors, with just horrific looks of defeat and exhaustion on her face. I found them amusing, especially as they were shown with music paying tribute to being knocked down and getting up again. I then adorned her with a "Lean Princess" sash, with which she was not at all amused with but did not have the energy to protest too much.

Shannon

I believe my response was, "Really?" When the model plant celebration kicked off in the conference room, we explained the extensive auditing process we had to go through to achieve our model plant certification. Allow me to elaborate to give the full picture. We ultimately had 13 days of auditing, including follow-up webcasts and 78 pages of feedback that we worked through. The evidence book was 113 slides. We had completed over 1,000 action items to get us here, managed 4,332 pull cards, created 300 plus standard work documents, driven 2,338 miles on the tugger, and built over 50 machine and operator balance charts, and I had taken 140 pages of notes from our Rick Harris days (front and back I might add).

It was finally our time to shine and prepare to celebrate all of our successes. During this time of the year, the CEO awards were also being given out. We won three awards that we were very proud of as well: Financial Performance,

Supply Chain Excellence, and Lean Excellence. It was definitely time to celebrate!

Kathy *Of course, we conducted tours, with our team members touting the various stages and accomplishments of the lean journey. I watched on as they spoke like seasoned practitioners explaining the tools and processes with expertise and how each one led to measurable business results. We had passed the learnings and applications of a successful lean transformation to the next set of manufacturing professionals.*

Shannon The tour went off without a hitch. The team did amazing, and I chimed in from the wheelchair when necessary. I couldn't have been more proud of our team's achievement. I remember thinking, "I knew we could do this!" then taking a deep breath to prepare for the next part of the day Kathy had planned.

Kathy *We had a meal for all of the team members on every shift. There was a large assembly before each tour in which I gathered the entire team underneath a huge LEAN MODEL PLANT banner that everyone in the plant had signed.*

I wanted to make sure that everyone in the plant knew that they were part of the accomplishment of becoming a Lean and Quality Model Plant. I told them how few plants received that recognition – and walked through the math. Out of 341 plants in our company globally, only 3 had achieved this distinction – which put us in the top 1% of plants. Only two were in North America, and we were the very first in our product group. After three years of hard work and perseverance, the business results were tremendous, and each and every one of them deserved to be so proud – proud for contributing ideas, solving problems, using new systems, and embracing change.

I gave a speech of how I fondly recalled my first job working in a car plant in the middle of the United States and remained close to manufacturing throughout my career. And although I had supported plants worldwide, I still believed in the excellence of American manufacturing. I told them about my deeply held belief that we can compete in the United States. What they had done in a plant that wasn't brand new or shiny, with some people who had worked there for a very long time, was proven to me that what I believe is absolutely true. And for that, I was sincerely grateful.

We turned down the lights. I had a big screen with yet another music video – Whitney Houston's "One Moment in Time" playing with employee pictures flashing across the screen, a patriotic theme celebrating the people who worked hard in that plant each and every day. There were cheers from the crowd as people saw their pictures or those of their friends'. My heart was full.

Shannon This music video was the most moving to date, and I will admit I teared up watching it. There are some special moments in life where the culmination of hard work, dedication, and resilience that you put in with the team around you finally comes to fruition and it feels really, really great. In addition to the pictures of the team, the video showed all of the detail that got us there, and finally the results our efforts achieved.

In three years, this is what we did:

74% reduction in our injury rate

50% improvement in profitability

25% increase in sales

16% improvement in productivity

93% improvement in quality defect reduction

45% reduction in work-in-process inventory

54% reduction in lead time

(Boom! Drop the mic!)

I mean, wow! Even now, I'm still blown away by what our team did. We had proven that the process Kathy and Rick Harris asked us to follow, to have faith in, not only worked but yielded remarkable business improvements. This transformation also created a fantastic culture of transparency, engagement, and empowerment among all of our employees. I am forever grateful to have been a part of it. Besides the tools, process improvements, and technical skills I developed, I discovered the type of leader I wanted to be. And on top of all of these accomplishments, I welcomed a healthy baby boy, Beckett Michael, into the world two weeks later!

Kathy *It has been six years since this epic business transformation was punctuated by this great celebration. As Shannon and I put the finishing touches on our account of this adventure, we are proud to say that all three of the plants we transformed are still running. We both moved on to other career opportunities shortly after this, but we never moved on from each other.*

Shannon Our bond is strong. We still generate brilliant ideas in the hot tub and find ourselves incredibly amusing. We have built a trust in each other that could never be replaced.

Kathy *We achieved great results by working hard, being true to ourselves, and helping others realize the greatness that is inside each and every one of them. We took our jobs very seriously, but ourselves not so much.*

We never wavered from who we were and we never apologized for wearing the most fabulous shoes ever to enter an industrial setting. As we left the offices and headed into the plants, the world in which we flourished, we always wore those steel toes proudly.

Index